HOW TO WIN IN CHINA

Business and Negotiation Strategies Revealed

Stephen P. Turner

L & T Publishing
Austin

L & T Publishing

4301 W. William Cannon Road
Austin, Texas 78749

Dedication and Special Thanks

This book is dedicated to my wife, Xi Li, for opening my eyes to new worlds and for unwavering love and support. To my parents, Marian and Jack Turner, for providing me with the lessons need to excel. To my mother for teaching me to never give up. To my father for teaching me to be fearless and to always do what is right.

Sun-Tzu once said...

> If a general follows my [methods for] estimations and you employ him, he will certainly be victorious and should be retained. If a general does not follow my [methods for] estimation and you employ him, he will certainly be defeated, so dismiss him.

ACKNOWLEDGEMENTS

I would like to thank my advisor and trusted friend, Dr. Clay Robarchek and his wife, Carol Robarchek, for their continued support, patient guidance and friendship. Their friendship has contributed to my personal and professional development. I would also like to extend my gratitude my advising committee; Dr. Art Rohn, Dr. Robert Lawless, and Drs. Dharma and Deema deSilva, for their wisdom and guidance. Thanks are also due to my readers, Li Xi, Jack Turner, Louise Burton, Tze Chao, Shaolin Zhang, and Gang Guo for their precious time, honest opinions, and wise suggestions. Special thanks are also extended to my wife's family and friends, in China, for their generous assistance during my fieldwork in China.

I also want to thank Michael Shores for applying his 20+ years experience of working with China and Asia in writing the Foreword. Additionally, I need to thank Stephen Anderson for his copyediting and proofreading and Robert Kauffman and Holly Robinson for their contributions and creative eye in cover design.

Forward

In my view, China is like a lottery and everyone is looking for the winning ticket where the grand prize is a 1.3 billion person market with a $4 trillion economy. Most foreign companies view China with a low budget investment strategy and a massive potential payout. The reality is that most companies end up just like most lotto-ticket buyers, with losing tickets. Of course, there are a few who break even and get their money back, fewer actually make a small profit, and even fewer win in China. Every year, more and more companies buy their ticket ignoring these truths because they are mesmerized by the jackpot! What these companies don't realize is that the ones that do make it typically didn't do it on their own without some serious guidance and sound strategy.

From my experience of doing business with Chinese for over 20 years, I've come to understand that companies can claim the prize of successfully doing business in China and that China can be a winning ticket for foreign business of all sizes, but to access it, the companies must understand the people, economics, politics, history, and business strategies of their Chinese partners and competitors. This is where most companies fail or fail to make a profit because they don't understand that buying the ticket is only the first step. To really WIN in China, foreign companies need a strong team that not only understands their own product; but more importantly understands how the Chinese do business, how they think, and their decision making process. With over 50 centuries of business practices and culture behind them, they've learned to be cautious of everybody and everything.

I have learned a great deal about the Chinese people and probably even more important is that I have learned more about myself. I have especially learned how Greek in nature our thought processes are in having spent most of my adolescent years growing up in the United States. When I say Greek I mean that we typically have more of a black and white view of events in life. The Chinese have a much more holistic view and see things through a greater than/less than mentality. With this type of mindset you have to pay special attention to everything that is said because it is all important, but some things just mean more than others and sometimes what is said is not actually what is meant.

Several years ago I was visiting a Hon Hai factory with over 300,000 employees in China and my American business associate hosting my meeting made a rather odd statement after our meeting. I should also add that his Chinese counterpart at their Company was also educated in the US and was very familiar with Western culture. The then odd statement that my American business colleague made to one of my comments after our initial meeting was "Yes, Michael, that is what he said but it's not what he meant". *I was perplexed and for years I didn't totally understand this statement. But fast forward and I find myself quite often using this same state-*

ment and of course I totally understand what it means now.

I first met Stephen through the Richardson Chamber of Commerce in Texas when he was working with KOTRA, the South Korean Investment-Trade Agency, in the Dallas office. One of the first things that struck me as odd with Stephen was how well he synced with the Koreans, like his group had been working with them for years. I later found out that he only knew a few words in Korean and didn't pronounce them correctly. As I got to know Stephen better over the years, I found his knowledge on China and Asia incredible. I'm talking about real knowledge; knowledge that makes a difference, knowledge that helps WIN contracts and make projects successful. I have been able to gain much insight from him over the years and, as you know, knowledge has to be applied in order to really become wisdom and that's exactly what I have done.

This is why Stephen is the best person to write this book. China is an extremely dynamic and ambiguous place to do business where surprises can and do pop up anywhere at any time. Stephen's holistic approach helps bring stability to the process by providing the reader with a road map to really understanding the business client, from the cultural undertones of doing business in China, including their decision making process, political and economic systems, as well as business strategies, to negotiation strategies. In short, this is one of the best "how-to" manuals on doing business in China that I've ever read. He not only explains why you need connections, but his holistic approach explains how to establish and develop your own connections that will last a life time. He covers the importance in discovering and understanding the latent intents or hidden agendas of Chinese partners, which are often the "root cause" of why so many foreign companies fail in China.

Stephen spent years researching and analyzing data on China, including its history, politics, culture, and economy, as well as negotiation strategies and tactics. This book is a well-researched compilation of data that is laid out in a way that is easy to understand and comprehend. After reading this book, it will change how you view your Chinese counterparts and how you view all contracts and business alliances.

This is the first book that I've read that actually explains or ties together many of the moving parts regarding how to successfully do business in China. It covers management style to business priorities, to negotiation strategies, to cultural understanding, to market entry, and many points in between. Much like a great number of books and articles everyone reads on doing business in China, it also covers the importance of connections. The difference is that this book actually explains in detail "how-to" establish your own connections and develop them over time rather than relying on 3rd party connections, such as a bank, law or accounting firm. As we've all experienced, once the third party is out of the picture, then you can feel very much alone and exposed in an environment that can, as an example, suddenly raise very specific local taxes, or introduce new and sudden Chinese owned competition.

One of the unique qualities of this book is that it's a must read for anyone at any level doing business with or wanting to do business in China. It covers every enterprise level from Fortune 500 to SMEs (Small and Medium Size Enterprise). At the top of the enterprise level, this book discusses the importance of understanding national development priorities, marketing and connection strategies to legally win contracts. At the other end of the spectrum, this book covers the importance of truly understanding Chinese culture and the decision making process. One of the key factors that Stephen discusses is the need for a market entry plan with an exit strategy. It is very important to know when to continue in China and when to cut and regroup so you can try again later. Many companies will have market entry strategies but leave out the exit strategy.

For everyone involved in the negotiation process, this book is a must read. Stephen discusses the negotiation styles of the Chinese that are unlikely to change for decades to come. He explains the importance of understanding your counterpart's goals and objectives, even the hidden ones. To walk away with a win/win scenario from the negotiation table, you need to understand what you won and what you paid for. In China, because they embrace ambiguity, especially on their end, it can be very difficult. Stephen helps you understand what is really going on so you can bring it into focus. Additionally, he discusses many of their strategies and tactics that are used during the negotiation process. To help with this, Stephen even suggests that you have mock negotiations and play both sides to better understand your position and your counter parts.

Overall, this is an excellent written book that tends to be written as a strategy manual, which it is, rather than a narrative of personal accounts. The objective view provided by this method and his holistic approach is exactly the perspective executives need to make key financial decisions. Based upon my experiences in China and Asia, this book has brought me a great deal of enlightenment that was missing. Going forward, I know that my personal dealings, our company's dealings, and our client's dealings will benefit from knowing "How to Win in China."

I love the Chinese culture and the Chinese people and I don't play the lottery. Actually, I strongly suggest you don't either so get some guidance with China or don't play.

Michael C. Shores
CEO
New China Ventures

Corporate Peer Reviews

Turner identifies challenges incisively. In doing so, he points to opportunities, and then describes approaches to solutions superbly. He respectfully understands impediments to success that both Western and Chinese participants bring to potential and existing business ventures. For Westerners' benefit, he clearly understands myriad Chinese complexities that "latent intents," which both communist and imperial systems fostered, affect business relationships and goes on to map paths to successful initial strategies and, also, to satisfactory resolutions of failed plans. For both Westerners and Chinese, Turner thoughtfully describes the inter-weaving that successful ventures require. Even better, because he grasps the significance of development over time, Turner effectively describes the weaving process for the ambitious, goal-oriented and success-dependent organizations. Read "How to Win in China" once, and expect to re-read it as China becomes more important to your success!

E. Patrick Jenevein III
CEO

CURTIS MATHES CORPORATION

With having crossed the Pacific over a hundred times, two things stand out the most when doing business there; first is to adapt to their world, don't expect them to adapt to yours, and always prepare, prepare, prepare before leaving the ground. A cultural advisor is just as important as the attorney, accountant and the airplane! Stephen's book should be in your back pocket.

Patrick Custer
CEO

LOCKHEED MARTIN

EXCELLENT MESSAGE!!!

Understand and respect your customer's culture in order to experience success!
I have found that most organizations do not pay attention to culture; in fact, expats are frequently sent into environments completely naive to the culture into which they must locate and conduct business.
Some aspects of the book I especially liked and with which I could identify were:

- The significance of the sense of balance which influences some many aspects of operating in China.

- Special dishes – it seemed that every meal in which I participated had to include sea cucumbers!!!
- Knowledge of Chinese history is important – an important resource.
- Corruption – know it exists and is lurking for the unsuspecting.
- Importance of Sun-Tzu – thought process important.
- Economic power of Chinese throughout SE Asia – Thai-Chinese, Malay-Chinese.
- The negotiations section was very good.
- Agree with the odd number philosophy!!

Paul T. Bergander
International Business Development

HILLWOOD, A PEROT COMPANY

WOW, what an awesome book! It hits all the critical components of doing business in China without making the book as long a Chinese history...he expertly describes the Chinese Culture and his definitions of the elements of balance of guanxi, mianzi, keqi, and renqing are concise and right on. He hits all of the important components such as political, legal, economic, and historical which form the foundation for negotiating (and re-negotiating) strategy.

Mr. Turner's definition of the roll of the Cultural Translator is right on. In negotiating with the Chinese, you need a trusted person who will "guide the negotiations towards an atmosphere that will facilitate and foster communication to establish trust between the parties."

Steve Boecking, AZS
Vice President, Business Development

CESSNA AIRCRAFT COMPANY

"How to Win in China is a comprehensive review of cultural and historical considerations that are behind any project in China, especially one using a joint venture. This review is an excellent place to start for anyone doing business in China, and as such makes it possible for the cultural translator to provide meaningful value deeper than an initial introduction."

Gordon Vieth
Vice President, Sales

PEERLESS MFG. CO.

The concept of the 'cultural translator' is such a critical factor in my business strategy for China. No matter how much attention we place on developing a good cost position and profit strategy, our chances of success are limited if the social perspective is not addressed properly.

Our goal is to establish business in China for the long haul and that will only be possible if we can balance the four cultural complexes to build respectful, lasting relationships.

David Taylor
Vice President, Business Development &
Asia Pacific Operations

GE EMBEDDED COMPUTING

Name a market that has a growing base of sophisticated and disposable income oriented consumers that is larger than the Pan Asian market. Europe is expensive, tired and broke. Africa and Latin America are years behind. Asia, powered by China, still looks like the next and closest continually promising market.

With that said, would you like to know and have advantages in building a successful attack plan to grow and sustain business in China? Tremendous lessons are covered on this topic by Stephen Turner, founder of Bing Fa Consulting, a group dedicated to building and driving business growth in Asia with a special emphasis on China. The book *How to Win in China*, is a very incisive look at skills you will need to hone and utilize if your quest is to be a success.

Mr. Turner addresses the subject as if it were a sequel in the "Indiana Jones" series where clues are given, CULTURAL TRANSLATORS are introduced, and a history lesson serves as the backdrop. It's unfortunate that more works on this type of topic don't take that approach.

This effort gives the reader a game plan to follow for conducting new missions or sustaining old ones in China. For example, if I were a multinational executive looking after China and I read this book, I'd want to quickly scrub my current and ongoing plans against themes of understanding cultural motives—the importance of Keqi, Renqing, Guanxi, and Mianzi.

I viewed the book through my perspective of having sold in Asia with several multinational companies including a role as Product Leader in High Speed Computing, Imaging and Graphics for General Electric's Embedded Computing Group. In my role I supported sales teams in Asia and India. My preference was to support my sales teams in China because of many points made in this book. My sales team in China respected knowledge and experience in selling high technology products vs. inexperience and an MBA in an irrelevant area. They appreciated an understanding of their customs and approaches to eating and building trust. Topics such as these are well defined and reviewed using examples by Mr. Turner.

James Falasco
Global Accounts Manager

Table of Contents

Preface

This research attempted to develop a systematic approach on how to develop a strategic advantage during international business negotiations through the use of a Cultural Translator. It was established, through prior research, that cultural conflicts are a leading cause for international joint venture failures. Additional research also indicated that international business negotiators who understood their Counterpart's mindset (i.e., how they are culturally programmed to act and react to situations, which includes in-depth knowledge of their cultural complexes and negotiation strategies and tactics) were successful in their negotiation process. These findings were also supported by my fieldwork in China.

The research concluded that companies wishing to successfully conduct international business should consult a Cultural Translator prior to the start of the negotiation process to assist the negotiating team throughout the entire negotiating process and the operations team throughout the life of the operation. This research focused mainly on International Joint Ventures, but the application of these findings holds true for any type of international operation from sales office to manufacturing plant to joint venture to wholly-owned venture.

Chapter 1

The Problem

Understanding Your Overall Goals is Key to Achieving a Strategic Advantage

There have been numerous publications written concerning international business theories and practices, for example, in economics[1], management[2], international business[3], marketing (Engholm 1994), and accounting (Clydesdale 1986). Reporters (e.g., Mann 1989) and business consultants (e.g., DeKeijzer 1995, Burstein 1998, Chu 1991) have also generated publications in this area. In addressing business in China, these publications focus on everything from how to conduct business in the "Chinese Triangle" to the economic reach of the "bamboo" network. The approach common to most of these publications is to provide international managers with an enormous amount of economic information, including market size, investment strategy, and business possibilities in a foreign country, while only providing a brief description of the cultural uniqueness of the country. The information contained in these publica-

---

[1] In economics–for example, there are articles by Wing 1997, Lardy 1992, Woo 1997, Weidenbaum 1996, Rohwer 1995, Dunning 1997, and Irvine 1997.

[2] In management–for example, Mathur 1987, Tan 1996A, Tan 1996B, Weidenbaum 1996, Trompenaars 1998, Wartick 1998, Autenrieth 1995, Miller 1999, and Hoskins 1999.

[3] In international business–for example, Kroeniger 1998, Ming 1998, Binder 1998, Contractor 1997, Rugman 1997, Robinson 1997.

tions is valuable, but its utility is limited because understanding the cultural traits of a target country is the critical factor to successful international business (Zeira 1995).

There are numerous studies showing that understanding culture is the key to successful international mergers, acquisitions, and joint ventures (e.g., Miller 1999, Hoskins 1999, Ning 1998, and Zeira 1995). In 1995, an article in the International Executive by Zeira estimated the failure rate of international joint ventures (IJVs) to be from 24 to 50 percent. Zeira attributed this failure rate to cultural differences arguing that "Organizational leaders often find it difficult to ascertain the latent intent or hidden agenda of potential foreign partners, and when they do venture jointly, they often find it difficult to share control mechanisms or to understand each other when cultural differences appear or environmental changes occur" (Zeira 1995:374). According to another study, 75% of the companies that have experienced such failures believe their business alliances failed because of an incompatibility of country and corporate cultures (Dutton 1999:36).

Much of the current business literature is designed to direct companies to new markets by pointing out market size, their key industrial areas, and easy ways to enter the market. They do this because it is well-understood that international managers need economic information to decide whether or not to enter a new market. To enter and compete successfully in a new market, however, they also need cultural information. These same publications seldom provide the useful cultural information that international managers need to address the most common problem with international investment: understanding the latent intents and hidden agendas of companies and their potential foreign partners. Instead, these publications address cultural issues by telling international managers simple "canned" answers, such as the Chinese term *"guanxi"* means "connections," or "back door" and that you need this to do business in China (Engholm 1994). These simple answers, however, don't address the serious and complicated cultural issues that are the causes of conflict, and that generate hidden agendas and latent intents.

Causes of Conflict

The key to solving many conflicts is finding and addressing the sources of the conflicts. International joint ventures (IJVs) are no exception. My research has indicated that there are two common sources for the cultural conflicts associated with IJVs (Miller 1999, Hoskins 1999, Ning 1998, Zeira 1995). The first cause of cultural conflict within IJVs emerges during the establishment stage; it is the lack of a common goal for the international partners. The other common cause of cultural conflict occurs within the corporate culture of IJVs themselves, and is associated with enculturation/avoidance, and sharing control mechanisms/transparency.

A Common Goal

Each company involved in an IJV has its own individual goals and purposes for its participation, and, these are not always directed to the betterment of the newly formed IJV. In fact, the IJV is usually just a means of reaching the individual company's larger overall goal.

A study published by the International Finance Corporation and authored by Robert Miller (1999) compared IJVs between industrial countries (ICs) and developing countries (DCs). He found that the top reasons why their IJVs were considered failures were conflicts in goals. The study found that ICs look to invest in IJVs mainly due to the DC's government regulations preventing independent investment. The IC's companies are hoping that, in time, the DC will relax their regulations and allow the IC's companies to go it alone. This is the current case with China.

Although China has opened up considerately since 1979 and its regulations on IJVs have eased in recent years, China still hampers the IC's access to internal markets. China does this by requiring most of what is produced within China by these IJVs to be exported. By the end of 1996, the government had approved about 280,000 Sino-foreign companies, and 140,000 companies were in operation. These companies have contributed about 13% of China's total fixed assets but the output of foreign companies' only accounts for 7.2% of the total Chinese industrial output. The import and export volume of IJVs, however, accounted for 47% of the total import a nd export volume of China (Binder 1998). As these numbers indicate, this could be a problem for the IC's companies, if their goal is to enter the Chinese market.

Conflicts occur because the companies involved are courting each other for completely different reasons. The IC's companies are generally looking for a local partner that can offer local expertise, which includes:

- Familiarity with local customs and conventions,
- Assistance with problems in managing the local environment,
- Knowledge of the legal system and government regulations,
- Familiarity with local product market and distribution channels,
- Knowledge of labor conditions

These were the most important contributions anticipated by the IC's companies from the local partners in DCs. Other contributions anticipated by ICs would include; sharing the cost of risk-taking, providing relevant contacts with the governments and elsewhere, uses of existing facilities, and more effective use of technology.

The DC's companies, on the other hand, have different expectations in mind when they want to venture jointly with an IC company. The most important anticipated contribution that the DC's companies were looking for from their industrialized partners was technology. Other anticipated contributions included access to management know-how and to export markets.

In addition to these differences in expectations there are also conflicting goals. As stated earlier, the number one reason for foreign companies to take on a local partner is to conform to government regulations. The ultimate goal of the foreign partner is to gain access to the local markets. The ultimate goal of the local partner is usually to increase sales through access to international markets.

The "Causes of Conflict" section began by saying that the key to solving many conflicts is to find and address the source of these conflicts because one source can result in many related and unrelated problems. This is why conflicts over goals are difficult to overcome because they are part of a larger picture. The IC's companies are usually Multi-National Companies (MNCs) that have a complete global strategy. A single IJV or even a single country is only one part of their entire global strategy. The MNCs are looking for access to sell products to the local markets. They generally are not looking for another IJV to manufacture products for export to other markets because this might interfere with other IJVs that they might have in other countries. On the other hand, the local partner already has access to the local markets and their goal is to expand into the larger international markets.

Miller's study (1999) illustrates these differences between companies when it comes to their anticipations and goals for IJVs. Miller argues that these differences are the latent intents and hidden agendas that are the main causes for the failure of IJVs. These hidden agendas and latent intents become the catalysts for a corporate culture that promotes mistrust among the employees from different countries, because part of their job is to ensure that the other side does not discover their hidden agendas and latent intents (Miller 1999).

Table 1.1

From the Perspective of the
Industrialized Countries Companies

Expected Major Local Partner Contributions	
Knowledge of Local Politics	70%*
Knowledge of Government Regulations	68
Knowledge of Local Customs	68
Knowledge of Local Markets	65
Provision of Financing	58
Local Reputation	58
Access to Local market	54

*Percentage of IJV sample where category was specified. Respondent could specify more than one category. (Source: Miller 1999:23)

Table 1.2

From the Perspective of the
Developing Country Companies

Major Foreign Company Contributes	
Process Technology	74%*
Product Technology	72
International reputation	70
Provision of Financing	65
Management Know-how	59

*Percentage of IJV sample where category was specified. Respondent could specify more than one category. (Source: Miller 1999:23)

Corporate Culture

Each company involved in an IJV is going to bring to it some of their own people, as well as their own company's way of conducting business, or "corporate culture," because they accept it as the way to conduct business. This brings together different groups of people with different corporate cultures into one company. The result is often cultural conflict.

In a study conducted by David Montgomery, professor of marketing studies at Stanford University, and Takehiko Isobe, associate professor of marketing at the University of Marketing and Distribution Sciences in Kobe, Japan, examined 1,148 overseas subsidiaries of Japanese companies found that enculturation in IJVs is a leading source of cultural conflict. Their study found "that the greater the influx of managers from the home country into a subsidiary, the more poorly it performed" (Dutton 1999:36). The subsidiaries performed poorly because with the influx of foreign managers came an influx of their ideas on how to conduct business the "correct" way. This type of corporate forced enculturation by one party means that the other party needs to practice avoidance to prevent cultural conflict from occurring and to ensure the IJV will be a success. If one party decides not to adopt a policy of avoidance in the face of another party's attempt to enculturate the organization, then the result will be additional cultural conflicts which, left unchecked, can and often does cause IJVs to fail. There could be any number of reasons why companies would rather not take an avoidance position in the face of enculturation. A leading reason for a company to reject the avoidance position can be found in the "hidden agenda". If there was a hidden agenda or latent intent involved in the establishment of the IJV then neither side would adopt an avoidance position in the face of enculturation because that would not allow their company to move forward with their hidden agendas.

The other major cause of cultural conflicts in IJVs occurs when there are multiples of bosses, concepts, and agendas for each party involved, because they cannot seem to share the control mechanisms within the IJV. This makes control difficult to enforce, since the decision-making authority is divided. In addition, this situation makes companies less transparent, meaning that they are more willing to hide agendas and intents if they believe that the other partner(s) don't share their same goals. A study entitled, "Learning and Performance in International Joint Ventures: A comparative Case Study," found that once companies obtained a controlling interest over the IJV, the more transparent they became to the other partner(s).

The IC companies believe that since it is their technology, their cash, and their know-how, all they need is access to the local markets. The IC companies therefore believe that they should be the ones in charge of the IJV. The DC companies on the other hand have a different perspective. They think that since they already have access to the local markets, and understand the laws, the government and cultural customs, that they should be in charge of the IJV. They are only looking to the IC to up-grade their technology and to gain access to international markets or to cash. Since the IJV is based in the local country, they feel they should be the ones in charge. This is the problem; both groups want to be in charge and to manage the IJV because it will allow them to control the situation and promote their own agenda, hidden or not.

That corporate culture is an issue when it comes to IJVs has recently become accepted, but there are few companies that are addressing it as a serious issue. According to Satish Sanan, the Chairman, President and Chief Executive Officer (CEO) of IMR Global, they examine 70 to 80 companies before acquiring 3. Sanan believes that "If the business cultures fit well, you can overcome the other obstacles" (Dutton 1999:37). Their approach is simple: get to know who your partner is before you put millions of dollars on the line.

Case Study: Omron
Understanding the Importance of
Culture to Performance

The goal of this book is to discuss how to successfully conduct business in China and internationally through the understanding of the importance of culture. The following case study (*Management Review* May 1999: 34-38, by Gail Dutton.) illustrates the key role that culture plays in international business. The case study illuminates two important areas regarding corporate culture. The first is how Omron established a core corporate cultural structure. Second is the importance of local participation and point of view.

Omron: A Global View

Omron, based in Kyoto, Japan, is a global corporation that, several years ago, went through a transformation. The executives at Omron, who had always assigned Japanese to head its offices around the world, realized that their growth did not depend solely on Japanese markets. They began to rely on more local expertise at their international offices. This mixing of Japanese and local expertise began blending the local experts into its organizational culture. Omron did not stop at just including local experts in to the operations. In 1999, they established English as the corporate language. This meant that everyone within Omron spoke English at all official meetings, including the board meetings in Japan, and all the correspondences were in English. They standardized the software to eliminate incompatibility issues and developed a global knowledge database and held global planning meetings in its offices throughout the world. All of this increased the smooth flow of communication at all levels and decreased the chances of miscommunication.

One of the most important benefits of these changes was that the company, from top management down, took on a global way of thinking that understood that business problems don't have "one right answer." This means that "they [Omron] and its companies are no longer tied to one business model or way of thinking and can use the best practices from throughout the world to respond to local challenges" (Dutton 1999:35). According to John Stopford, professor of international business at the London Business School, this ability will improve their business performance. Stopford stated, "The ideal is to have a team in which all are cosmopolitan in outlook, as this saves the costs of great argument trying to persuade the parochial members that best practice at home is not necessarily the best for the present and future" (Dutton 1999:35).

My purpose in presenting this case study was to illustrate how cultural differences and/or ethnocentric points of view can affect a company's everyday performance. Omron was able to improve performance by allowing their international managers to participate in the global planning and manage their local offices within the host country's cultural norms. To do this, they removed some of the cultural barriers that were causing the conflicts, mainly the failure to show respect toward the locals by listening to their advice. This allowed them to utilize the local talent's business know-how and troubleshooting abilities within the local offices and within the entire Omron operation. This also meant that Omron executives were now open to suggestions and ideas regarding business development. In addition, by removing the cultural conflicts, they were able to identify and respond to new opportunities quickly, thus achieving an improved strategic advantage.

The Definition of Culture

The approach incorporated in this book is premised on the importance of culture. It is critical, therefore, to understand what culture is and how it works. Anthropologist Victor Barnouw (1985:5) defined it as "a way of life of a group of people, the complex of shared concepts and patterns of learned behavior that are handed down from one generation to the next through the means of language and imitation" (Barnouw 1985:5).

This definition is the foundation of the theory discussed in this book because it implies that there is integration and cohesion in a way of life and the concepts and life patterns of a particular group of people are, for the most part, stable over time. It also means that individuals within a cultural group have similar decision-making processes (Barnouw 1985), which I call "the cultural mindset."

The purpose of culture is to provide "canned" solutions to most of life's challenges. In short, it "provides the means for coping with the world; mastery of these methods increases one's sense of confidence" (Barnouw 1985:6). This confidence is backed by bodies of doctrine about the world in the forms of religious traditions, philosophies, and folklore (Barnouw 1985).

This is the true power of culture. People seldom question the way things are in the culture into which they are born. The power of culture is so great that people perform actions without realizing the thinking patterns behind the actions, for instance, how people greet each other, dress or how early or late they are expected to be for a business meeting. These are culturally programmed actions and reactions shared by most of the people within the society. The reason why they have the same actions and reaction is that they have been exposed from birth to certain patterns of behavior or ideals that they have been taught to believe are correct. The result is that their cultural mindset has been programmed to think and reason within their culturally defined parameters, which are very difficult to change. Their behavior, therefore, is predictable and can be anticipated (Barnouw 1985).

Cultural Translator

To solve cultural operational and managerial issues, international managers need to possess a certain world view, according to Vijay Govindarajan. Govindarajan (Dutton 1999) is the professor of international business and Director of the "Global Leadership 2020" management program at Dartmouth College in Hanover, New Hampshire. He points out that the components needed to make up a positive world view would include holding "multicultural values, basing status on merit rather than nationality, being open to ideas from other cultures, being excited rather than fearful in new cultural settings, and being sensitive to cultural differences without being limited by them" (Dutton 1999:35). He adds that executives with a true global mindset will give all ideas the same credence, even ones from developing nations (Dutton 1999).

I believe that Govindarajan is correct in his assessment of the qualities that are needed for all international managers. I also believe, however, that in order to solve the cultural conflicts that occur while establishing an international operation, international managers will need to possess two additional characteristics. First and foremost, they should have a sophisticated understanding of culture and how it works. Secondly they will need to be proactive in gathering cultural data, especially regarding the similarities and differences between the cultures.

By "proactive", I mean that they will actively re-search the other culture in question to develop an understanding of the cultural mindset. This type of person is more than just an international manager; he or she is a Cultural Translator. As such, the best people qualified to be Cultural Translators are cul-tural anthropologists because they already have a high level of cultural understanding that can be used to obtain an understanding of their counterpart's cultural tactics during the negotiation process in es-tablishing the IJV. They are also qualified to assist with the corporate culture issues surrounding encul-turation and the sharing of control mechanisms after the IJV is established.

The Cultural Translator's job is first and fore-most, to obtain a sophisticated understanding of the cultural mindset of the culture in question. Then utilize that knowledge and understanding to build a team with a global mindset. This team will then as-sist in finding the right partner. In addition, he or she will guide the negotiations towards an atmos-phere that will facilitate and foster communication to establish trust between the parties, thus minimiz-ing the need for hidden agendas and latent intents. The Cultural Translator's job is to "facilitate com-munication by acting as a translator, by assisting in cross-cultural understanding, and by serving as a third-party facilitator who can conduct informal ne-gotiations in the hall, dining room, or office where the real deal is often structured" (De Keijzer 1994: 176).

Why a Cultural Translator?

Cultural Translators should be utilized in any situation where cultural awareness and understanding plays a key role, from establishing an IJV to managing the cultural conflicts caused by differing corporate cultures. They can be useful during the negotiation phase of contracts to design human resource policies that can smooth the operations of joint ventures, mergers, or acquisitions where differences in national or organizational cultures may be creating operational issues.

In China, bureaucrats involve themselves in Sino-foreign projects; therefore, it's critical for a foreigner to understand why these politicians want to be involved and what the motivations are behind their interests. There are several reasons that motivate Chinese politicians to become involved in foreign business deals. One has to do with the regulatory privileges that a partnership with a foreign firm will bring to their organization. A second reason is profit. A foreign partnership will bring with it foreign exchange. A third reason is to gain respect. An official who has been able to establish good relations with a foreign firm will gain respect and authority (direct or indirect), over higher-level officials. In addition, if an official is able to bring in a cash-rich foreign partner, then he/she will be able to receive reciprocal favors from other related organizations (Engholm 1994).

Not only can Cultural Translators by understanding the local cultural structure (i.e., governmental, political, legal, economic, and religious structures), help to protect a company from bureaucrats who think they have found the "mother lode," they also can protect the company from "fool's gold." China is a huge market and to most companies is a gold mine of opportunity just waiting for them to tap it. Sometimes gold miners found themselves filled with false hope from "fool's gold." Cultural Translators will be better able to distinguish between the enthusiasms for a real gold mine of an opportunity and the "fool's gold" of one based on the Chinese characteristic of *keqi* or politeness. *Keqi* mandates that the Chinese be polite, even if they have no interest in the foreign company's proposal. This culturally mandated Chinese enthusiasm can give international managers the false hope of a great opportunity.

A Cultural Translator will not be able to solve all the problems that companies experience when conducting business internationally, however through his/her capacity for cultural understanding, he/she will be able to avoid or eliminate many of the cultural problems that have caused IJVs to fail in the past.

The Cultural Approach

The cultural approach utilized in this book is a simplified version of the more detailed approach used by cultural anthropologists. The anthropological approach is designed to collect very detailed information regarding how a culture works. There are three methods of data collection that are most common: participant observation, interviews, and library research. Participant observation involves the anthropologist living with a group of people and participation in and observing their day-to-day way of life. The interview method generally used while conducting participant observation, is used to ascertain specific detailed information regarding various specific aspects of a way of life, such as religion or philosophical beliefs, the role of government, and the economic situation. The library research is an attempt to utilize various sources of cultural information to identify a people's cultural characteristics. The anthropologist analyzes the data from these various sources in an attempt to understand why people behave as they do, why certain events happen, what their effects on society are, and why they are important to a group's way of life.

In answering these questions, the anthropologist is, among other things, trying to understand the society's cultural mindset, a people's cultural perspective. Understanding the other's cultural perspective is vital because just knowing about a unique cultural trait, such as, in Chinese culture, the term *mianzi* (face), meaning social position or social self-worth, is not enough to allow one to understand its true power within the complex of Chinese Culture. In order for Cultural Translators to fully understand the meaning behind the Chinese term *mianzi*, they first need to understand the Chinese mindset and the role *mianzi* plays in it. It is only by developing an understanding of their mindset that a Cultural Translator can achieve a strategic advantage over their Chinese counterpart by understanding how the Chinese think and why.

This approach is also known as the "holistic" approach because it examines the various parts of a culture to understand how they fit together to make up the whole culture. Cultural Translators don't have the time to utilize the same methodologies used by anthropologists, nor is it necessary for them to do so. Anthropologists have already conducted research on over 3000 societies. The Cultural Translator can conduct library research focusing on religion, philosophy, government, norms and customs, and the economic system. Almost all the information that he/she will need has already been published; the Cultural Translator just needs to access it and be able to utilize it.

The key to understanding another culture starts with locating this relevant cultural information, and library research will typically be the main method used by Cultural Translators in researching another culture. A few excellent places to start would be anthropological journals and publications that focus on global studies, most of which can be found in the local university's library. Another source is the local department of anthropology. Some professors are cultural consultants, who may teach classes regarding the culture in question, and they will also be an excellent source for locating additional sources of information.

Other non-anthropological sources would include the local World Trade Center/Council, the local US Chamber of Commerce, as well as other chambers, such as the Asian American Chamber of Commerce. In addition, the public and local university libraries have journals like the International Executive, Foreign Affairs, and Journal of International Business Studies. The internet is now a great source for accessing research papers or for finding web pages that are reference sources that let people know where to find specific papers and reports. In addition, The

World Fact book and the National Trade Data Bank are excellent for providing an overview of an entire country, including some relevant cultural data.

A good university library is the best source for the widest variety of authoritative publications regarding cultural information. Obtaining the broad perspective required by Cultural Translators, means reading publications on several subject areas. As a place to begin doing research would be business travel books that briefly cover a broad range of topics, such customs, religions, history and important sites. These are valuable as a head start because some of them will explain why these are important, thus giving insight on where to focus the cultural research.

There are also publications that cover country specific news, current events in the form of journals and quarterlies. Knowledge of current events will keep international managers abreast of the current situation and, perhaps more importantly, help them anticipate what might happen in comings weeks, months or even years. Trying to understand another culture takes time and is an ongoing process, but once an initial mass of understanding is achieved, new learning will come much easier.

Although the ideal approach would be to examine every aspect of a culture, the reality of the situation is that Cultural Translators don't have the time. They should utilize a strategic management approach that prioritizes, concentrates, and executes a given plan. They should concentrate their efforts on important areas that were discovered in their preliminary research. To operate effectively in the international business arena, the Cultural Translator must understand the cultural environment he/she is entering by means of purposeful preparation ahead of time. Failure to consider the cultural perspective can, and has, led to misunderstandings, miscommunication, lawsuits, and generally an undermining of goals (Ferraro 1994).

This section has discussed how international managers should prepare when conducting international business, but all this effort will be wasted unless what is learned during this process is successfully executed. In my research, I came across people who actually took the time to read at least an introductory book on how to conduct business in the country they were planning to visit, but then they did not follow the advice. A case in point is a young woman who was several years out of college and her company sent her and a few other colleagues to their Japanese office for a week to assist with a research project. In anticipation of this trip, she read an introductory book on how to do business in Japan. The book covered various topics from gift exchange to going out after work, both of which are important parts of socializing in Japan. I asked what gifts she took with her to give to her Japanese counterparts. She explained that it was the same company; therefore, they did not need to take any gifts. Then I asked if her Japanese counterparts took the time to take her and the rest of their party out every night after work. She said that they did, but the company paid for it and that it was typical in Japanese culture to go out every night after work. I agreed, but I pointed out that it was not typical for them to go out with her and her group, and they did so because Japanese culture dictates that they do, so they did. Then I inquired who was paying for all of this, and she informed me that it was the company. I then asked where the money was coming from, her office or the Japanese office's budget. "Of course, the Japanese budget" she responded. I then asked if the Japanese counterparts gave them any gifts when they left. She said that they did, but they were just little token gifts and company paid for them.

In short, her group flew for about 17 hours to go to Japan on a business trip. They participated in areas of Japanese culture that they found convenient for themselves, such as going out for nice dinners and accepting gifts from their host. They choose not to participate in the inconvenient side of Japanese culture, such as taking small tokens of gratitude to their hosts. She did not understand that such tokens are a symbolic gesture by the guest as a sign of appreciation to their hosts for going out of their way to ensure that the group had a successful and enjoyable visit. "You do not understand. We are the same company. We do not need to take gifts." She interrupted.

Another problem facing Cultural Translators is the American ego. It has been my experience in American companies that people tend to talk and act as if they know everything they need to know about the task at hand. (This seems to be especially true for people who have MBAs and engineering degrees.) There appears to be some unwritten rule that they cannot ask for assistance or suggest that they don't know something. Any answer, even a wrong answer, is better than no answer in their rulebook. To the Cultural Translator, however, this must not be the case. The ego needs to remain in check at all times since one of the most important jobs that a Cultural Translator has is asking questions, especially "why?"

These are some of the problems facing international business. People can do the research on another culture, but unless they utilize their newfound knowledge, acquiring it has been a waste of time. In improving cultural relations, it is absolutely necessary to follow as closely as possible the other culture's cultural norms, without "going native." It is imperative for the Cultural Translator to maintain his/her cultural identity and self-respect; however, important information and opportunities will be lost by refusing to participate in cultural customs, such as drinking alcohol during the host dinner. For example if a person who is Jewish or Muslim politely refuses to eat pork at a host dinner, what is lost by offending the host will not be gained back in respect for standing for what she/he believes. In situations like these one should inform the host ahead of time to prevent any miscommunication or embarrassment. It is important to remember that cultural acts, such as the host dinners, are important for helping to tear down the walls that cause misunderstandings, cultural prejudice and stereotyping; therefore participation is essential. Such events serve a purpose, which is to enable both sides to see over the walls, thus allowing the parties involved to see what they have in common. If the walls remain up, then they can only see their differences, which drive them apart instead of bringing them together. If this culturally-informed approach is applied and executed properly, it will result in a better level of cultural understanding, which will lead to trust and will increase the likelihood of success.

Culture and International Business

The idea of using culture to facilitate international business seems only logical, considering that international business is defined "as those business activities of private or public enterprises that involve the movement across national boundaries of resources, goods, services, and skills" (Phatak 1989:2). By definition, doing business internationally means companies are going to encounter different cultures. Companies will inevitably experience a certain level of cultural conflict during the normal course of conducting business internationally. This situation, however, is manageable through cultural understanding. According to Dr. Dharma deSilva, Director of the Center for International Business Advancement at Wichita State University, an understanding of latent cultural characteristics is a prerequisite to effective inter-cultural communication.

Dr. deSilva is not alone in his view. Other researchers are producing publications that promote using culture to improve international business. For instance, Edward T. Hall (1959, 1966, 1976), Geert Hofstede (1997), Gary P. Ferraro (1994), Steven L. Wartick and Donna J. Wood (1998), Fons Trompenaars and Charles Hampden-Turner (1998), Gail Dutton (1999), Michael Solt (1995) and Yoram Zeira (1995), all promote the importance of understanding cultural nuances. Michael Solt's (1995) research found that, "awareness of cultural differences is necessary in order to understand managerial behavior and achieve success in international business transactions" (Solt 1995:415). Solt maintains that "As the global nature of the business environment increases, interactions between individuals from different cultures also increase, both in frequency and complexity. A growing volume of international business naturally generates a greater frequency of cross-cultural interactions. As firms accumulate more foreign manufacturing and marketing operations, cross-cultural interaction becomes more intense and continual" (Solt 1995:415). Solt's research in China found that, "...understanding the value system employed by PRC managers can lead to improved staff development and smoother operation. Unfortunately, Western managers appear to lack the understanding necessary for operating successfully within the PRC culture" (Solt 1995:416).

John Stopford, professor in international business at the London Business School, agrees that a global outlook will improve business performance. He also adds that it is ideal to develop an entire team with this global perspective (Dutton 1999).

David Montgomery, Professor of marketing studies at Stanford University, and Takehik Isobe, Associated Professor of marketing at the University of Marketing and Distribution Science in Kobe, Japan, found that cooperative management is also profitable. Their research found that companies, who rely more heavily on both local and international expertise and management methods, rather than strictly applying their home country management styles, were more profitable. This is the same approach that the Omron Corporation adopted (Dutton 1999).

International Business

There are several reasons why international business can be critical to companies; these include profits, global strategy, product development, new technology, and many more. In most cases the ability to conduct international business requires some type of direct foreign investment. Here are some comparative figures: "Direct investments abroad by US companies at the end of 1996 were in excess of $259 billion, and those by foreign companies in the US amounted to more than $209 billion" (Phatak 1989:1). To put these numbers into perspective, in 1986, the value of all the final goods and services produced by the national economies, (or gross national product [GNP]) of every country in the world, excluding the ten wealthiest, was less than $235 billion (Phatak 1989). This is about 25 billion less than what American companies alone invested abroad. These numbers are impressive and growing. During the 1980s about 80% of American exports were conducted by less than 1% of all American companies (Ferraro 1994).

To companies investing abroad, the international market is important for many reasons—gaining access to new customers, achieving a larger market share, or lowering manufacturing costs. Another important reason why companies invest abroad has to do with the international business theory "international product life cycle." Manufacturing companies are eager and willing to invest in foreign countries, even in the second and third worlds, because this will extend the life cycles of products, which allows them to achieve better economies of scale, access to new customers, and a better return on investment.

The International Product Life-Cycle

This is how investment in developing markets works: Company OGA, for example, makes a CD player to be sold in the US, Japan, and Western Europe. It sells well and in about 18 months, it has been replaced with a newer model. The older model is still a good product, just slightly outdated in the first market countries due to new features like MP3. It can then be sold in the developing markets more cheaply because the company has already achieved a favorable return on the cost of development, marketing, and production. By distributing the product to the second and third markets, the company is extending the product's life cycle from 18 months to possibly three to five years. This extension allows the company to receive a larger return on its investment. In addition, by manufacturing the product over a longer period of time, the company is able to achieve a better economy of scale on the product and on future products.

One of the hidden secrets of an extended product life cycle is the built-in second and third markets for future products. In the first market, the US, Japan, and Western Europe companies have loyal consumers and a brand name. This can also be true in the second and third markets. If consumers bought the first version of the product, they will probably also purchase the upgraded version when it hits their markets. The company has increased its market share of a single product by investing abroad, and has lowered production cost per unit by achieving a better economy of scale. In addition there is generally cheaper labor, land, buildings, and power for companies that create IJVs, as well as tax incentives.

The company initiating the IJV is not the only winner. By expanding into new foreign markets a company will also bring with it new technology, better paying jobs, management experience, and a host of other extra benefits. The developing country receives a larger tax base, an increase in the number of skilled jobs and trained workers, and an increase in the development of the infrastructure, to list just a few benefits.

There are also potential negative consequences surrounding foreign direct investment in and/or trade with impoverished (and not so impoverished) areas. The new technology and the better paying jobs take people away from their traditional method of earning a living, be it farming, raising cattle, fishing, or working in state-owned enterprises. Offering better jobs and more pay may upset the social and economic balances. An excellent example of this situation is Russia. Russia's social and economic balance collapsed due in a large part, to the rapid movement of their skilled workforce from lower paying jobs with the state-owned enterprises (SOEs) to the private sector for better pay. The result was the collapse of the Russian economy (Woo 1999).

What anthropologists worry about are the long-term effects of such changes. What happens if the new plant closes and the farmers were not able to plant their crops? In a traditional extended family society, like China, what happens if the children move away from home to the city for the better pay-ing jobs? Who is going to take care of the parents and grandparents? These are serious and real problems currently in China. This situation has caused the Chinese government to write into law, article 15 and 22 of their constitution. These articles state, respec-tively, that it is the responsibility of the child to take care of the parents and, if the children are not able to take care of their parents, then the responsibility falls on the grandchildren. Family unity and taking care of the parents and grandparents are major is-sues in China, as well as in most developing socie-ties. Foreign direct investment is much needed to bring a better quality of life, a better standard of liv-ing, human rights, and much more. It can also be quite devastating to the social wellbeing of a society if it is not managed properly.

The American Mindset
Regarding International Business:

One of the consequences of developing a cultu-rally sensitive mindset is the self-examination of the international manager's own culture. Ferraro (1994) calls it cultural self-awareness. It is a necessary step in becoming culturally aware of other cultures. Fer-raro explains that culturally different people view the world based on their cultural understandings. When a person is culturally sensitive he/she can also see the influence of their own culture on their own thought processes and behavior (Ferraro 1994).

A study of 127 US firms with international oper-ations found that these American corporations be-lieve that the education of international managers needs to focus primarily on technical training (Ferraro 1994). This mindset of American companies could be a leading reason why "75% of companies believe their business alliances failed because of an incompatibility of country and corporate cultures" (Dutton 1999:36). A company can send all the technical people it needs to explain their product and how it works; but this does not assist in overcoming the cultural conflicts that ultimately cause IJVs to fail. Professor Howard Perlmutter of the Wharton School of Business put it best: "If you have a joint venture with a Japanese company, they'll send 24 people here to learn everything you know, and you'll send one person there to tell them everything you know" (Ferraro 1994:15). Other studies have shown that the failure rates of international businesses result from their inability to understand and adapt to foreign ways of thinking and acting rather than from technical issues (Ferraro, 1994). In contrast, in a study on the criteria for managerial advancement in China, technical business knowledge ranked only fifth out of the seven criteria (Solt 1995). This study, in conjunction with the other supporting evidence, highly suggests that when a company expands into international markets technical knowledge is not as important as the knowledge of cultural norms such as, in China, the complexes of *mianzi* (face), *keqi* (politeness), *guanxi* (connections), and *renqing* (cultural obligation). In the face of this overwhelming evidence that the high failure rates of IJVs is culturally based, US managers still continue to insist on more technical training for their international managers.

Tung and Miller's (1990) study suggested that Americans are ethnocentric in their management style and don't consider the importance of other aspects of international business. Their study suggests that the root of the American ethnocentric management style is the assumption that *their* ethical values are absolute and universal. The American ideal for ethical behavior is a set of universal ethical values that all cultures follow at all times. This would help to explain why American managers stress technically oriented people. They believe that there is only one ethical way to conduct business—theirs. Therefore, the only factors in question are those surrounding the technical aspects of the product. The result is that the vast majority of IJV failures are not because of technical issues. They fail because of cultural issues, most of which center on trust and ethical behavior. The point of this is that ethical standards are *not* universal and this needs to be addressed prior to trying to establish operations around the world. This is especially true in China where business contracts change as the business environment changes. US companies and managers with their absolutist business mentality are not responding adequately to the globalization of business.

Chapter 2

Chinese Culture

Understanding How a Counterpart Thinks is Key to Developing a Strategic Advantage

The purpose of this chapter is to sketch an outline of Chinese culture. This will be accomplished by briefly examining their beliefs, religions and philosophies, because they define what the Chinese consider the parameters of acceptable and non-acceptable behavior, or the "norms of behavior." This chapter will also briefly discuss four key cultural complexes: *keqi* (politeness), *mianzi* (face/social worth), *guanxi* (connections), and *renqing* (reciprocity/cultural obligation).

Section One: Achieving Balance

Yin and Yang represent the principle of duality, where two forces hold the universe together and in balance. These two forces are positive (Yang) and negative (Yin) forces. In ancient Chinese thought, every aspect of nature is imbued with these two forces. It is believed that Yin and Yang must stay in balance and in harmony with one another for things to be right with the world: for crops to grow, for people to remain healthy and content, for governments to function, and for companies to prosper (De Mente 1996).

This concept of maintaining balance and harmony is fundamental to the Chinese cultural mindset and is supported by bodies of doctrine that are founded in traditional Chinese beliefs, philosophies, and religious teachings. These bodies of doctrine provide the Chinese with the "canned" answers they need to understand the mysteries of life, and to allow them to accept the good and bad things that happen in their lives. This belief in a balanced universe may seem esoteric to some Western businesspeople, but understanding it is crucial to understanding the Chinese. It is the function of the Cultural Translator to promote understanding of the principles that regulate the Chinese cultural mindset, and to show their role in Chinese thought process and behavior (De Mente 1996).

The Influence of
Religious and Philosophical Beliefs

Every morning throughout China, there will be people lighting incense, offering food and drink to their ancestors and making offerings at other religious shrines in the hopes of guaranteeing a favorable day. Many small businesses maintain little Buddhist and Taoist shrines, and there may be pictures of the proprietor's ancestors with incense burning in front of them. This is maintained in the hope of assuring good fortune and of warding off bad fortune. These shrines can even be seen in Chinese-run business here in the United States. These beliefs and religious acts go beyond offering tokens to ancestors; these rituals are conducted to maintain balance throughout the day. Many Chinese ask for positive assistance from various religious deities and ancestral spirits because they believe that there are negative forces acting against them.

Feng Shui is a set of beliefs that are associated with the physical world and movements of the sun and moon (De Mente 1996). *Feng Shui* has incorporated various elements from different Chinese religions and philosophies into its current practice. The famous nine-turn bridge is specifically designed to prevent evil spirits from following a person across the water. The bridge is designed with nine right-angle turns in it because it is believed that evil spirits can only travel in straight lines, therefore if a person changes direction nine times, then evil spirits cannot follow them across the water. There are nine turns because the number nine is also important in Buddhism, where it is believed to be a lucky number. It is considered lucky because Buddhist pagodas always have an odd number of tiers, generally seven or nine (De Mente 1996).

Beliefs surrounding lucky numbers are not uncommon throughout the world; in America the number 13 is associated with bad luck. It is considered a very unlucky number and some hotels don't even have a 13th floor, even if the building has more than 13 floors. The number even generates a bad luck day, Friday the 13th. However these numbers are not believed by most Americans to have any real influence on their lives.

Among the Chinese, however, especially among the older generations, beliefs are taken very seriously. This is especially true if they believe that bad fortune has fallen upon them. For one seeking to do business in China, these beliefs need to be taken seriously, because during negotiations of a business deal, the Chinese may wish to have a master of *Feng Shui* called in to offer advice on what steps the company needs to ensure good fortune (De Mente 1996).

To the Chinese, these and other beliefs are an integral part of their way of life. There are, for example, things that should never be given as gifts, especially things associated with or reminiscent of death and separation, such as clocks and fans. The word for clock is pronounced the same as the word death, and the word for fan is pronounced the same as the word for separation, therefore clocks and fans are inappropriate as gifts because they imply bad fortune for the recipient.

The color red can also be filled with problems. Traditionally it is associated with greatness and power in China; however, to write a person's name in red is a sign of bad fortune, since the only time a person's name is written in red is on their tombstone after he/she has passed away. Prior to 1949, tombstones were generally purchased with the names of the husband and wife already engraved into the headstone, prior to death. Then, when one of the individuals died, their engraved name would be painted in with the color red. This signifies that the person is no longer living. (In print, a person's name with a black box around it is also a symbol that he/she was no longer living.) The color red should, therefore, be avoided on business cards, because of these connotations. The printing on business cards should be only gold or black.

Printing a name in black with a box around it may seem an unlikely mistake, but one should watch out for reports that might list officers with a black border around the person's picture and with their name below the picture. One should also avoid black borders on dinner place settings.

Another area where Western businesspersons need to take care is in gift giving. The color of gift wrapping paper to avoid is white, because in this function it is also associated with death. In the past, corpses were wrapped in white burial shrouds. White gift wrapping paper symbolizes this burial cloth to the Chinese.

These are just a few examples of potential mistakes that are associated with various beliefs. There are countless others. What is important is that most Chinese do believe in these beliefs, or at least they generally react according to their cultural conditioning. The Cultural Translator, therefore, seeks to recognize and communicate such potential cross-cultural problems to those considering doing business in China.

A Philosophical Overview

According to *Chinese Philosophical Thought* (Shaw 1991a), the Chinese have a 5,000-year history and, over this time, they have developed a body of philosophical thought, which they call, "Sages and Hundred Schools of Thought." Some of the best known of these schools are Confucianism, Buddhism, Taoism, and Legalism. The Chinese have been able to combine the ethical ideals of these different schools of thought within one culture because the philosophies are not necessarily exclusive in their teachings.

Confucian teachings, for instance, followed an ethical philosophy that stressed social order through hierarchy, structure, and rituals. Buddhism, on the other hand, teaches self-control and humility, while Taoists adopted a more artistic belief system that strives to be in harmony with the natural way of the universe through yin and yang (Shaw 1991a). From these teachings emerged a Chinese culture that stressed three ethical ideals: benevolence, ceremony, and filial piety (Shaw 1991a).

These three ethical ideals emerged as part of one culture because they complement each other. The Chinese people consider "benevolence" as an inborn sense of what is moral and right. While they associate rational forethought and self-restraint with "ceremony." They believed that the purpose of a "ceremony" is to maintain a society's ethical order and the harmonious atmosphere needed for group development. Under this framework, the Chinese believe that "benevolence" and "ceremony" do complement each other because they are inherent in man's nature (Shaw 1991a).

Filial piety is a special ethical ideal to the Chinese; for it is through this that they show their respect for their parents as their origins of life (Shaw 1991a). In China, it is the children's responsibility and duty to support and assist their parents. They are also responsible for their welfare and upkeep when their parents become unable to support and care for themselves (De Mente 1989). This is also written into the Chinese Family Law. Article 15 states that parents have the right to demand support from their children; and, in addition, Article 22 goes further by stating that grandchildren are responsible if their parents are unable to fulfill their duty to their parents (De Mente 1996).

Even though the children should do everything they can to support their elders, the elders are ones that are generally in charge. Since one of the primary pillars of the traditional Chinese way of life is the importance of age and seniority, the young are taught to respect and obey their elders, particularly their fathers and male figures in positions of authority. The elderly are still highly valued in China for their wisdom, experience and historical knowledge. This "filial piety" has been a part of Chinese culture for a long time and was the basis for Confucius five distinct relationships (De Mente 1989).

Confucius (Kung Fu-Tzu)

Confucius' teachings are not, strictly speaking, a religion. They focus on how individuals should interact to maintain a harmonious order within a society. He presented a way of life stressing relationships and obligations that were structured and organized through a strong sense of ceremony, hierarchy and authority. This order is based on five distinctive relationships, Ruler to Subject, Elder to Younger, Husband to Wife, Father to Son or Parent to Child, and Friend to Friend. These five relationships formally established a hierarchical order illustrating how a society should be organized. Confucius stated, first, that subordinates are obligated to follow their leader, the Emperor. The other four relationships stress the organization, structure, authority and hierarchy of the family and close friends. By defining the relationship of the ruler and subjects first and then focusing on the structure of the family, he defined the role of the family and its place in society.

Confucius, whose real name is Kung Fu-tzu, lived from 550 to 470 BC, which means that the Chinese have been passing down his thoughts from one generation to the next for over 2,470 years. His five distinct relationships are deeply rooted in Chinese culture.

Confucianism, however, is not alone in shaping Chinese culture. As discussed earlier in this chapter, there are various aspects of other belief-systems that have also been incorporated into Chinese culture, especially elements of Buddhism, and Taoism.

Today, Chinese culture is a combination of key aspects derived from these various philosophical teachings. From these various teachings and schools of thought, four cultural complexes have evolved that ensure balance is maintained within the society (Waley 1989). These cultural complexes are *keqi* (politeness), *mianzi* (face), *guanxi* (connections), and *renqing* (reciprocity). These, in turn, are reflected in the cultural characteristics of benevolence, ceremony, hierarchy and authority, and filial piety that allow Chinese to maintain a sense of balance in their society and in their lives.

Section Two:
How the Cultural Complexes Work

This section will illustrate how these four very complicated cultural complexes are utilized to ensure that balance and harmony are maintained within society. These four complexes– *keqi* (politeness), *mianzi* (face/social worth), *guanxi* (connections), and *renqing* (reciprocity)–are difficult to explain individually because they are completely interdependent and work much like a system (see figure 2.1) to ensure harmony or balance within the society.

Mianzi (Social Self-worth)

In this interconnected and interdependent circle of Chinese cultural complexes, *mianzi* (social self-worth) is one of the hardest to define. "*Mianzi* has been described as a sense of social status, what a person thinks of himself or herself in relation to all other people" (De Mente 1989:61). It is also a form of "social prestige," meaning something that society bestows upon a person and it is measured in terms of how high one is in society, in one's wealth and power (De Mente 1989). There are many definitions for *mianzi*, but they all have an underlying theme of being something that is bestowed by society upon a person, but it can also affect the entire family. I prefer to define it as "who a person is within the society," or "the sum of the person's social worth." Good *mianzi* means that people can trust that person. It is like a reputation, but much more and far more serious (De Keijzer 1992).

In addition, if *mianzi* is lost (i.e., lost due to an insult or a lack of trust), it must be restored by a means that will bring with it social respects. This usually means an act of revenge. A person's *mianzi* must be restored because it represents who a person is within Chinese society. If they have lost their *mianzi*, then they have no social identity. To the Chinese, a person's *mianzi* is everything at all times, everywhere, even among total strangers. To lose one's *mianzi* in front of others is a major insult that must be restored. In all relationships, personal and business, it is critical to the Chinese that they maintain *mianzi* and avoid offending the *mianzi* of others. "Failure to preserve the *mianzi* of others is tantamount to robbing them of their social status and bringing great humiliation on them" (De Mente 1989:61).

Keqi: (Politeness)

To ensure that *mianzi* is maintained at all times there is the second cultural complex that states that people must maintain a high level of politeness toward each other at all times, this cultural complex is called *keqi*. *Keqi* (politeness) is what ensures that *mianzi* is maintained at all times because it regulates people's societal behavior through humility. When *keqi* is referred to as "being humble," it means not only personal humility, but also downplaying the status of one's family, friends, employer, and so on. When it is used to describe behavior, it means being polite, courteous, modest, humble, understanding, considerate, and well mannered. These are the qualities that are needed to protect one's own *mianzi* and everyone else's *mianzi* around them. To cause someone to lose *mianzi* would also be an act against *keqi*, thus entailing a loss of one's own *mianzi*. *Keqi* is the pressure that Chinese society applies to an individual's behavior to ensure that he/she does not offend another, thus *keqi* helps to ensure that *mianzi* is maintained at all times (De Mente 1989).

Mianzi and *keqi* are interconnected cultural complexes that regulate an individual's social behavior. *Mianzi* ensures that a person is benevolent, humble, while *keqi* ensures that they are benevolent and follow the culturally defined rules of hierarchy and authority.

Guanxi (Connections)

The third cultural complex is *guanxi* (connections) and it is the cultural aspect most frequently discussed by many Western authors. They have often defined *guanxi* as "connections," but it is much more than just "connections," as this section will illustrate. *Guanxi* is the ability to use one's *mianzi* and *keqi* to establish a social network of close and trusted friends. The purpose of this social network is to strengthen an individual's ability to ensure balance is maintained within his/her way of life. This is accomplished by utilizing the members of a person's social network or *guanxi* for favors both great and small. This can include everything from avoiding trouble with the police or state to winning business contracts. It could also be used for something as small as delivering a letter to the post office. A person's *guanxi* literally affects every aspect of his/her way of life, and it is completely based upon a person's *mianzi* and ability to maintain *keqi*.

Western business people perceive this cultural complex as a "backdoor" to special business deals, including gaining favorable conditions in winning business contracts. The Chinese, on the other hand, have a different perception of this cultural complex. They believe it to be an essential part in maintaining balance within their way of life and society. A failure to conform to the expectations of any of these complexes would bring a loss of *mianzi* upon someone, which would be a violation of *keqi*, and could result in the loss of favors either from this person or the entire *guanxi* network as an act of revenge. From the Chinese perspective, allowing a friend (a person within their *guanxi* network) to win a business contract is a small price to pay to ensure balance in their life. This is how the Chinese maintain balance, one person assisting another for assistance in return at a later date. This is a serious matter because as one on my informants told me, "*guanxi* is how things get done in China, let your friends do the work."

Due to this cultural structure that utilizes a social network to accomplish anything from everyday tasks to special favors, it cannot be stressed enough that proper behavior, along the lines of benevolence and humility, is the key to a successful relationship or *guanxi*. Ceremony also plays a key role in *guanxi* especially when it comes to business deals with foreign partners. The best example of this is the first host dinner given by the Chinese for the future foreign partner. The host dinner is the first official meeting of the officers and it is a ceremony. Its purpose is to see if the potential partners possess the abilities to function within the Chinese social structure. In other words, do the future partners possess qualities similar to those of *mianzi,* and *keqi?* They do this through a ceremony because a ceremony requires rational forethought and self-restraint, qualities needed for *mianzi*. The dinner also provides an opportunity for the Chinese to observe the potential partner for qualities needed for a harmonious group development. The Chinese do this because they need to make sure that the foreign company is not going to make them lose *mianzi* and that they will reciprocate when it comes to *guanxi*, because in China, *guanxi* is power, and with power comes responsibility.

This power does not come from one person; it comes from one's family and from knowing a group of trusted friends who are willing to do special favors or requests for that person based on their *mianzi* with that person. At the very center of the *guanxi* network is the person's family, which also includes their extended family. All family members are trusted and are a part of one's *guanxi* network. If one family member is powerful and has good *mianzi*, then his/her whole family has their *mianzi*. This also means that if an insult is given to one family member then it is an insult on the entire family. Additionally, if the insult is great enough, then it can affect everyone within the persons' *guanxi* network. The family shares in the humiliation caused by an insult delivered by one of its members because it was their responsibility to ensure that the children were properly enculturated. These insults or loss of *mianzi* can even affect a person with good *guanxi*, thus *keqi* demands that everyone be polite at all times (De Mente 1989; De Keijzer 1994). People within their *guanxi* network can be affected because they should have chosen their friends better.

Historically, this type of social system based on networks is common among impoverished peoples with weak justice systems. The Chinese put their faith in family members and a few close friends to protect themselves against injustice, dishonest practices, or mistreatment by others. This is why *guanxi* is power in China. The Chinese only trust people they know and who have established good *mianzi*. This is why host dinners and other ceremony type events are important to business dealings, because they establish *mianzi* and demonstrate *keqi*. The failure of a person or a company to establish good *mianzi* first could result in being mistreated or cheated, because they are without *mianzi,* which means they are without *guanxi.* Therefore, Cultural Translators need to be extremely careful with whom and how they conduct business (De Mente 1989; De Keijzer 1994).

Guanxi is not easily obtained because it takes time to develop *mianzi.* Thus the first step in establishing *guanxi* is *keqi,* meaning that the Cultural Translator needs to be careful not to do anything that would offend others or anything that will bring shame upon one's company or oneself. Sometimes this means keeping one's opinions to oneself. This will bring the Cultural Translator good *mianzi,* which is critical for the second step. The second step is to successfully develop *guanxi.* This can be accomplished by utilizing good *mianzi* to interact with a wide variety of people and organizations. It is necessary to develop *guanxi* with various people and organizations because it is needed at different levels of influence and points in life (Yefu 1991). Traditionally *guanxi* is established through kinship, schools, institutions, gender, and social class, rank and long-term familiarity with business associates (De Mente 1989; De Keijzer 1994).

Cultural Translators need to be careful with *guanxi* because it works on trust and *must* be reciprocated. Many Western authors have discussed the importance of *guanxi* in China, but they failed to emphasize that it is reciprocal. If negotiators for an American company want to utilize their *guanxi,* they need to be prepared to reciprocate, because if they don't, then they are not following the rules of *keqi* and *mianzi*, which opens them to acts of revenge.

The Chinese are able to utilize their *guanxi* networks because *mianzi* and *keqi* obligate their family and friends to assist. A failure to assist a family member or a friend would go against *keqi* and mean a loss of *mianzi*, therefore, to ensure balance in one's life people are obligated to follow the culturally established rules of *mianzi*, *keqi*, and *guanxi*. It is this dependency on cultural obligation or *renqing* that makes the complexes work.

Renqing (Reciprocate)

The fourth cultural complex is *renqing* (reciprocate) because it enforces the rules regulating *mianzi*, *keqi*, and *guanxi*. Figure 2.1 illustrates how the four complexes are interdependent upon each other to ensure balance.

Renqing is the expectation that people will follow the rules and behave properly. A failure to do so would mean that the social rules of *keqi* were violated, which would mean a loss of *mianzi*, which would mean that the person's *guanxi* network would also lose *mianzi*, which then causes the person to lose even more *mianzi*. *Renqing* is the cultural obligation that enforces these cultural rules because the four complexes are interconnected and interdependent. *Guanxi* is maintained through *renqing* and no *mianzi*, means no *renqing* because people will no longer have the cultural obligation to assist someone even within their *guanxi* network, if that person has no *mianzi*. The four cultural complexes are interrelated and they are the keys to understanding the Chinese way of doing things (Shaw 1991b).

There are two ways that *renqing* ensures that a person's cultural obligations are being fulfilled. The first is by a strong sense of cultural pressure to obligate a person to follow the norms that are associated with *mianzi, keqi*, and *guanxi*. The cultural pressure applied could mean the risk of losing *mianzi*, which in turn would mean a loss in social status and their *guanxi*. The second type of control is revenge. If the social pressure is not enough to regulate an individual's activities through the normal means of losing *mianzi* and *guanxi*, then the person whose *mianzi* was lost is obligated to perform an act of revenge, which will restore *mianzi* and bring balance back in to his/her life. Such a person is obligated to perform an act of revenge or he/she will become a victim to additional social pressures and will lose more *mianzi*. The act of revenge is an effective cultural weapon that ensures everyone follows the rules regulating the complexes of *mianzi, keqi*, and *guanxi*.

To make someone lose *mianzi* could cause an act of revenge that might be acted out the next day or in 10,000 days. This need for revenge stems from the long cultural tradition of not speaking directly or strongly regardless of the strength of the feelings involved plus the fact that any overt physical response was strictly taboo (De Mente 1989). People who understand the Chinese understand the importance of *mianzi*. This need for revenge occurs when their reputation or *mianzi* has been impugned or when they have suffered an injustice from anybody. Historically, there has never been any reliable justice system in China, and only people with *guanxi* had even limited protection against injustice. This left revenge as the only form of restitution. Due to the strong social sanctions against physical or verbal violence, the Chinese became adept at taking their revenge in more subtle ways (De Mente 1989). This could be at the hands of the original offended person or of any family member at any generation level from someone within his/her *guanxi* network. To the businessperson, this could mean the loss of a deal.

Figure 2.1

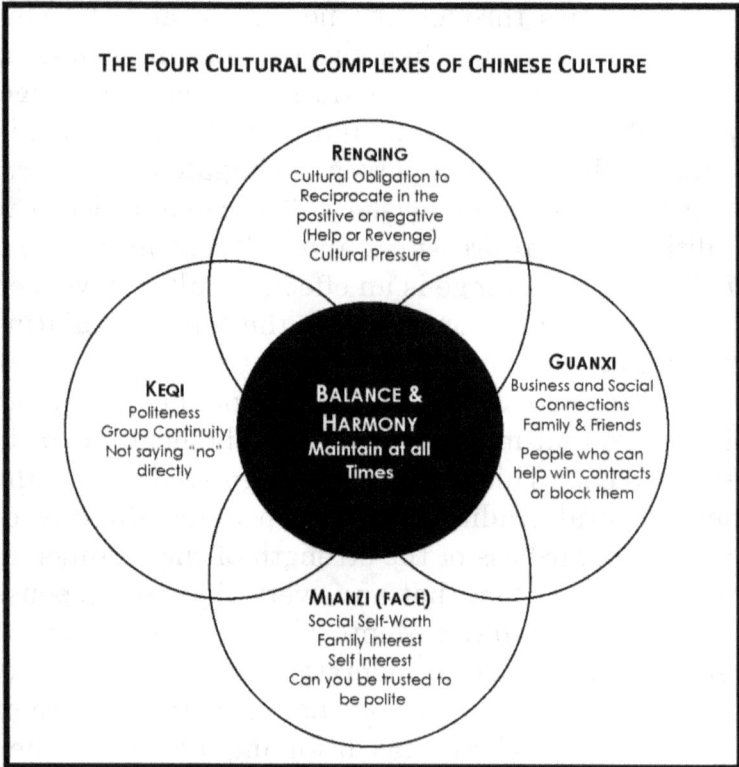

THE FOUR CULTURAL COMPLEXES OF CHINESE CULTURE

RENQING
Cultural Obligation to Reciprocate in the positive or negative (Help or Revenge) Cultural Pressure

GUANXI
Business and Social Connections
Family & Friends
People who can help win contracts or block them

BALANCE & HARMONY
Maintain at all Times

KEQI
Politeness
Group Continuity
Not saying "no" directly

MIANZI (FACE)
Social Self-Worth
Family Interest
Self Interest
Can you be trusted to be polite

The Cultural Mindset

If people were not culturally obligated to uphold the rules of the complexes then there would be a lack of harmony. *Renqing* is what ensures that harmony and balance will be maintained. The cultural traits of *keqi* and *mianzi* interact with each other because in order to obtain *mianzi*, a person needs to be able to demonstrate *keqi*. *Keqi* and *mianzi* are needed to obtain *guanxi* because the only way a person can develop *guanxi* is to have *mianzi* by demonstrating *keqi*.

Cultural Translators wanting to successfully conduct business in China need to develop a thorough understanding of the four cultural complexes, as well as, the ethical ideals of benevolence, ceremony, and filial piety. This will allow them to achieve a strategic advantage over their competitors because they will understand how the Chinese are culturally predisposed to think and react. This will give them a blueprint for how to approach the Chinese on most matters and, most of all, it will increase the level of trust between the involved parties because the will be demonstrating qualities of the four cultural complexes.

A Symbol of Balance: Food

One of the most important cultural elements to the Chinese is food. As one Chinese informant once told me, "America is the culture of sex, and China is the culture of food."

This chapter began by examining some Chinese beliefs, religions, and philosophies. These demonstrated that the Chinese need a sense of balance in their lives at all times. One element key in maintaining this balance is the family.

Symbolic evidence of this connection between family and balance can be seen in their attitudes toward food. The Chinese believe that their food must also maintain a sense of balance, much like a balance between hot and cold or Yin and Yang. They believe that the dishes they eat need to have a certain degree of balance with regard to color, aroma, and taste in order to promote their good health. Most of the dishes they prepare have three to five colors consisting of a combination of light green, dark green, red, yellow, white, black, or caramel. The aroma of a dish is provided by selected spices, mostly being scallions, fresh ginger root, garlic, chili peppers, wine, star anise, cinnamon stick, pepper, sesame oil, and dried black mushrooms.

The goal in Chinese cooking is to preserve the fresh, natural flavor of the ingredients and to remove any undesirable fishy or game odor. This also means that Chinese are not accustomed to the texture and odor of aged beef. They prefer fresh meat and this is why they will have live fish and other seafood, frogs, tortoises, and other small animals at restaurants. To remove fishy or gamy tastes, they use scallions and ginger, as well as soy sauce, sugar, vinegar, and other seasonings. These add richness to a dish by removing the fishy and gamy smell, but without covering up the natural flavor of the ingredients (Shaw 1991b).

The color, aroma, and flavor of the food must also conform to the most important concern of Chinese cooking: the nutrition of the meal. For the course to be balanced and nutritional, it must follow the harmonization of food theory developed by Yi Yin during the Shang dynasty. It takes into account the five flavors of sweet, sour, bitter, piquant, and salt in relation to the needs of five major organs of the body, heart, liver, spleen/pancreas, lungs, and kidneys. The goal is to promote and maintain good physical health (Shaw 1991b).

As stated earlier, Chinese food has a symbolic meaning in Chinese culture. It represents the coming together of family and friends with the goal of ensuring balance within their lives. The family members depend on each other to ensure balance, just as the dishes depend on the various spices to ensure that the color, aroma, and taste are balanced to give good health.

Since such food is an important aspect of Chinese culture, it is certain that during business negotiations there will be several group meals that the participants will have together. These dinners are very important and are called host banquets. This is the same as bringing the spices together to see if the dish will be a balanced dish.

Banquets

As discussed earlier in this chapter, Chinese culture believes in the importance of ceremonies, and business deals are no exception. One of the most important rituals of a business deal is the host banquet. This is a banquet put on by the Chinese side in honor of their guests. These banquets are intended to bring the various sides of a business deal together to establish fellowship, which is a key factor in doing business in China. These banquets take on a ritual character in how people are introduced, greeted, and seated. These are all factors that define the tone of the banquet as well as its seriousness. These banquets help to determine whether or not there is compatibility between the parties.

Since the banquet is very important to the success of the business deal, it is conducted like a ceremony; this includes a set of procedures the banquet will follow. Banquets are arranged on a per table basis, not on how many people are in attendance. Each round table will seat between ten and twelve people. The banquet will generally consist of four appetizer dishes, six to eight main courses, then one savory snack-type dish and a dessert (De Mente 1996). Key elements of Chinese banquets are not only the quantity and high quality of the food, but also the variety. Every banquet will have fish, soup, pork, fowl, and what I call a "surprise." The fish could be anything from shrimp to sea cucumbers. The soup can be anything from highly prized shark fin soup to something as simple as hot and sour soup. The pork can be prepared in many different ways, including roasting, where the skin is very crisp and the meat is tender, juicy and full of flavor. The fowl is usually duck, which can be cooked in many ways, including Peking Duck, which was President Nixon's favorite.

Then there is always a dish that I term the "surprise." There are two reasons why the Chinese serve a surprise dish. First, it is a "surprise" to the foreigner, not to the Chinese. They order special dishes that they would not usually be able to order, if the company were not paying for it. Some of these dishes require notice to be given several days in advance in order for the cook to obtain all the ingredients and to prepare it properly. Some examples of some of the smaller dishes that I have encountered would include drunken shrimp, where the Chinese river-shrimp are brought to the table alive in a bowl of wine. Then they are eaten alive. Another interesting dish is duck's bill, where the duck's bill and tongue are cooked in a heavy sauce and served as one piece with the ducks mouth wide open exposing the tongue. Some of the more interesting dishes would include snake, tortoise feet, scorpions, and a wide variety of small sea creatures. Most of these are displayed alive in front of the restaurant to allow the host to pick the ingredients for the meal, which ensures its freshness. These are a little difficult to eat at first, but with a little practice the banquets will go without any problems.

The second reason why the Chinese test the foreigners is to see if they are open-minded regarding Chinese culture and food. They know what dishes Americans are accustomed to eating and what they are not. This is a test to see if the guests are going to impose their American cultural ideals on them.

To the Chinese, this is a good test to see if the Westerners are going to make a good fit. It is a good idea, therefore, to inform the Chinese host, prior to the visit of any religious conflicts, for instance— Jewish and Muslim religious prohibitions on pork. This is very important because the Chinese eat a great deal of pork and it would be a loss of face for the host if pork was served and the guest could not eat it. The Chinese would take it as if they had insulted their guest, thus causing the Chinese side to lose face. It is also a sign of mistrust and incompatibility because, if one side feels so strongly about a situation as to cause the other party a loss of face, how will they act when it comes to other issues. What else might the foreign partner "forget" to tell the Chinese?

Another type of Chinese dining is a Cantonese style of eating called Dim Sum. It consists of small dishes or servings of a variety of different types of informal dishes, including pork and shrimp dumplings, chicken feet, cow intestines, and other delicious items. This is famous in Hong Kong and Guangdong province. It is also growing in popularity in the rest of the world, where there are Chinese. I was even able to enjoy Dim Sum at the Vancouver airport while waiting for my plane to Beijing.

Dim Sum was originally served as a brunch, but today it is served all day and all night, especially in Hong Kong. There are such a variety of choices that a person can be overloaded with these bite-size delights. The real purpose for choosing Dim Sum is to allow people to chat and eat casually for hours. It is a perfect opportunity to be sociable, make friends, and clarify business issues and negotiation points.

The underlying theme of food in the Chinese culture is the unity of ingredients symbolizes family unity. This is clearly seen in some dishes. For example, dumplings and hotpots, for example, involve the coming together of many different foods into a single flour wrap or pot. It also brings everyone together around a table, where they all eat from the same dish at the same time. The entire process of eating, from how the dishes are prepared to how they are eaten, is symbolic of Chinese family unity and friendship.

Summary

This section discussed the foundations of the Chinese culture by first examining the Chinese core concern with maintaining balance within their lives. Within a historical context of intense poverty and the lack of an effective legal system, the Chinese belief system evolved, including the four cultural complexes of *mianzi*, *keqi*, *guanxi*, and *renqing*, which developed to ensure balance, would be maintained within the society. This promotes a society that believes individuals must maintain a strong sense of self-control through a strong sense of *renqing*. This assists in maintaining the status quo. It also makes the family and close friends the only people a person can really trust. This combination has made the family the foundation for maintaining balance within Chinese society.

Chapter 3

The Chinese Political Arena

Understanding Your Counterpart's Political Arena
Helps in Defining the Cultural Mindset and is
Key to Winning Large Contracts

This chapter will discuss how political events, the Chinese Communist Party's (CCP) relationship with the State, and the legal system have reinforced the four Chinese cultural complexes that were discussed in the previous chapter. As Figure 3.1 illustrates, these three areas, which I call the political arena, have also reinforced a traditional sense of mistrust toward and fear of the CCP, the Chinese government, and authority figures.

The first section, "Political Events" will provide a brief timeline of political events that have occurred since the founding of the CCP in May 1921. There are two reasons why understanding these events is important. The first is that they illustrate many of the bad experiences that the Chinese people have endured under the CCP over the past fifty years. Secondly, these political events provide the Cultural Translator with a glimpse of how the political system in China actually works. The second section, the CCP's relationship with the State, discusses the roles of the CCP and the State in running the country. The last section in Chapter 3, the legal system, explores the history of the legal system and what it is today. These three areas should provide a general overview of the Chinese political arena by exploring its historical context, structure and function.

Political Events

The following is a timeline and brief explanations of political events that occurred between the founding of the CCP in 1921 and Jiang Zemin's instruction the People's Liberation Army (PLA) to sell off its 20,000 plus businesses in 1999. The purpose of this section is to sketch the important events that have occurred in recent Chinese history because they helped to define the cultural mindset and reinforced the four cultural complexes. In addition, this knowledge is useful because the Chinese hosts will be impressed to know that a foreigner has taken the time to learn a little about their history. This will go a long way toward establishing friendly contact. To the Chinese, it illustrates that the person has an open mind regarding China and her ways of doing things.

Figure 3.1

Chinese Political Arena

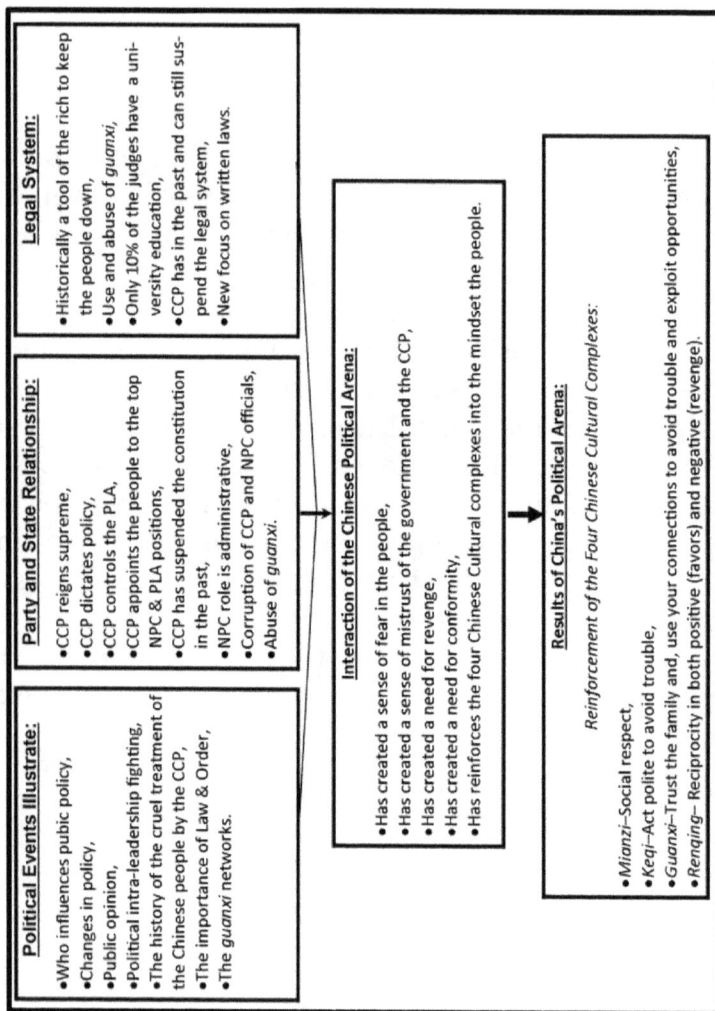

Political Events Illustrate:
- Who influences pubic policy,
- Changes in policy,
- Public opinion,
- Political intra-leadership fighting,
- The history of the cruel treatment of the Chinese people by the CCP,
- The importance of Law & Order,
- The *guanxi* networks.

Party and State Relationship:
- CCP reigns supreme,
- CCP dictates policy,
- CCP controls the PLA,
- CCP appoints the people to the top NPC & PLA positions,
- CCP has suspended the constitution in the past,
- NPC role is administrative,
- Corruption of CCP and NPC officials,
- Abuse of *guanxi*.

Legal System:
- Historically a tool of the rich to keep the people down,
- Use and abuse of *guanxi*,
- Only 10% of the judges have a university education,
- CCP has in the past and can still suspend the legal system,
- New focus on written laws.

Interaction of the Chinese Political Arena:
- Has created a sense of fear in the people,
- Has created a sense of mistrust of the government and the CCP,
- Has created a need for revenge,
- Has created a need for conformity,
- Has reinforces the four Chinese Cultural complexes into the mindset the people.

Results of China's Political Arena:

Reinforcement of the Four Chinese Cultural Complexes:

- *Mianzi*–Social respect,
- *Keqi*–Act polite to avoid trouble,
- *Guanxi*–Trust the family and, use your connections to avoid trouble and exploit opportunities,
- *Renqing*– Reciprocity in both positive (favors) and negative (revenge).

CHRONOLOGICAL ORDER OF POLITICAL EVENTS

1921 May	*Chinese Communist Party (CCP) Founded*
1923–1927	*The First United Front*
1923	*The People's Democratic Dictatorship (PDD) was created*
1927 March	'Report of an Investigation into the Peasant Movement in Hunan' by Mao is published
1927 Apr. 12	*Shanghai Massacre*
1927 Oct.	Establishment of the Jinggang Shan 'base area'
1931 Nov.	Establishment of the Jingxi Soviet, with Ruijin as its 'capital'
1932 Aug.	Mao replaced by Zhou Enlai as the political commissar of the Red Army
1934 Oct.15	The Long March begins
1935 Jan. 6–8	Zunyi Conference–Mao installed as general secretary of the CCP
1936	*Xi'an Incident*
1936–1941	*The Second United Front*
1941–1949	*Communist Revolution/Civil War*
1949 Oct. 1	*People's Republic of China founded*
1949 Sept.	*Chinese People's Political Consultative Conference (CPPCC)*
1956	*Hundred Flowers Bloom Campaign*
1958–1960	*The Great Leap Forward (GLF) headed by Mao*
1960	The Great Leap failed, causing struggle for political power
1965	Mao's ability to lead is challenged by P'eng Ten-huai
1966	P'eng Ten-huai dies in a plane crash on his way to Moscow

CHRONOLOGICAL ORDER OF POLITICAL EVENTS

1966–1976	*Cultural Revolution headed by Mao*
1978	President Deng Opens China's Economic Doors to the West
1978–1988	China has double-digit economic growth; people become rich
1987–1990	China experiences higher than expected inflation
1989 June	*The June 4th Incident or 6-4 Incident*
1989 June	*Jiang Zemin announced as the Party General Secretary*
1996	Deng Xiaoping Dies
1993 March	Jiang Zemin Elected, President of the People's Republic of China
1998	*Jiang removes all People's Liberation Army (PLA) influence from top CCP seats*
1999	*Jiang Zemin tells the PLA to sell off its 20,000 businesses*

The following are a few key summaries of political events from the list above. These events show a progression in how the political landscape can impact the Cultural Mindset. A Cultural Translator should follow the political landscape as well as the business one.

The formation of the Chinese Communist Party (CCP): May 1921

The CCP was founded in Shanghai, with Chen Duxiu as its first general secretary; Mao Zedong was one of the 12 founding members. All the revolutionary intellectuals were inspired by the social and political "ferment" in China, rather than being representatives of the working classes of the country (Christiansen 1996).

From these founding fathers of the CCP came a constitution, which outlined the CCP's role as the leader of the revolution and of the people's democratic united front (this description can be found in the Common Program of the Chinese People's Political Consultative Conference (CPPCC) and the Preamble of the Constitution of the People's Republic of China). This created the formal structure for the state that ultimately enabled the Chinese Communist Party to exert its control over the country by managing elections and making appointments to core posts (Christiansen 1996).

First United Front: 1923–1927

The First United Front occurred with the signing of the Sun-Jove Manifesto in January 1923 and lasted until the Shanghai Massacre of April 12, 1927. Initially, the Soviet government extended a hand to assist the Republic of China, which was headed by the Kuomingtang (KMT) party (a.k.a. the nationalist party), in reorganizing their government and party which included joining the KMT and the CCP (Christiansen 1996). The CCP members, however, had to join the KMT as individuals and not as a party. The overall reorganization of the KMT fell along Leninist lines and the members of the CCP took this opportunity to place some of their people in key positions, as well as to spread information about the CCP and to recruit new members (Dreyer 1996).

The People's Democratic Dictatorship (PDD) was created in 1923.

The PDD first came about during the First United Front in 1923, which united the communists and the nationalists. The Executive Committee of the Communist International believed that the CCP did not represent a large enough segment of the Chinese population. Therefore, in order to gain support, they suggested an alliance with the bourgeois classes to accomplish a "democratic revolution" first. This alliance created the People's Democratic Dictatorship, which united the anti-feudalism and the anti-imperialist groups with the CCP at various levels of Chinese society. Later, bureaucratic capitalism was added to the list of evils that must be eliminated (Dreyer 1996).

The CCP was able to gain the support of the Chinese middle classes and peasants by limiting the objectives of the "people's democratic dictatorship" to abolishing feudalism, imperialism and bureaucratic capitalism. The abolishment of "feudalism" also included doing away with the feudal system that held women in bondage (Christiansen 1996).

Doing away with Imperialism meant doing away with all foreign prerogatives in China, mainly by expelling foreign powers from territorial concessions in China and by fully restoring Chinese jurisdiction over foreigners in China. All rights bestowed on foreigners by unequal treaties were abolished. The most important implication was that the PRC did not inherit any international commitments, and that recognition of the PRC must be unconditional and not subject to renegotiations of old treaties, restoration of confiscated foreign assets, or guarantees of any sort.

Shanghai Massacre: 12 April 1927

In April 1927, there were armed labor union protests taking place in Shanghai. Chiang Kai-Shek, head of the KMT and the Republic of China, believed that only the nationalist army should be in charge of protecting the people, and, on April 12, the national army tried to disarm the unions in Shanghai. The CCP and the Left wing of the KMT supported the unions. Therefore, Chiang ended the First United Front, and the army killed many workers, members of the CCP, and Leftist members of the KMT. This drove the CCP underground and caused the Left wing to break off from the KMT, calling themselves the Wuhan coalition. The CCP and the Wuhan coalition joined together and the CCP was able to retain support among the "'national bourgeoisie" (Dreyer 1996).

Xi'an Incident: December 12, 1936

Chiang Kai-Shek, leader of the KMT, was kidnapped and then released on December 25, 1936. With his release, Chiang agreed to a Second United Front. (Dreyer 1996, Blunden 1991).

Second United Front: 1936–1941

The Second United Front came about due to the Xi'an Incident wherein Chiang agreed to stop attacking the communists, to give them "democratic rights," and to start making plans jointly to fight the Japanese. The CCP agreed to stop their armed attacks on the KMT and to rename certain areas of their organization to conform to the KMT's organizational structure. This included renaming the CCP's Red Army to the Eighth Route Army and placing them under the jurisdiction of the National Revolutionary Army (Christiansen 1996).

Between 1936 and 1941, the CCP created mass organizations that were designed to channel the energies of specific groups within the population to support CCP programs. The first of several programs the CCP started were elections followed by limited land redistribution and education reforms. The CCP was also stressing Nationalism and anti-Japanese sentiment to the working classes, which in time won their support. These programs were taking place in the CCP controlled areas in North China next to the Japanese controlled areas and far from the KMT controlled area in the south. The Second United Front alliance continued until 1941, when the real civil war erupted in China (Christiansen 1996; Blunden 1991).

Communist Revolution/Civil War: 1941–1949

The Civil War started in 1941, and when the Japanese surrendered to the Allied Forces in 1945, the civil war turned in favor of the CCP. This was significant because communist Russian forces were the first Allied group to enter China; therefore, they captured much of Japan's heavy machinery and guns. They then gave this equipment and weapons to the CCP. By the time the KMT troops fought their way to Yan'an (the capital of the CCP) to capture it, the people's support was drifting towards the CCP due to very high inflation and corruption within the government and the KMT. The civil war ended with the defection of two KMT generals to the CCP, including the general protecting Beijing. The Civil War ended on October 1, 1949, when Mao Zedong rode into Tiananmen Square and proclaimed the founding of the People's Republic of China. The KMT fled the mainland to Taiwan where they continued their government of the Republic of China (Christiansen 1996; Blunden 1991).

Chinese People's Political Consultative Conference (CPPCC): September 1949

The CPPCC was a symbolic representation of the united front against feudalism, imperialism, and bureaucratic capitalism. This conference was important because it established the PRC by imposing a set of laws in late September 1949. It was also a critical step in a formal, systematic process that established the government of the People's Republic of China (PRC). Then on October 1, 1949, from the rostrum in Tiananmen, the Chairman of the CCP, Mao Zedong, proclaimed the People's Republic of China (Christiansen 1996).

Yundong or Hundred Flowers Bloom Campaign: 1956

"Let a hundred flowers bloom, let a hundred schools of thought contend" was the slogan that launched the Yundong in 1956. Mao and the CCP invited the intellectuals, artists, and the managers of its economic enterprises to review the work of the communists in rebuilding China after the success of the revolution. It is Christiansen's theory that Mao wanted validation from the masses of the CCP's progress. What Mao and the CCP received instead was serious criticism regarding many of their policies.

This criticism was not what Mao was expecting and the campaign came to a sudden stop. A short time later most of the outspoken individuals were arrested and sent to jail (Christiansen 1996).

This was a brief event, but a very serious one because the CCP and the State had established a constitution, laws, and a legal system that the CCP then disregarded to arrest the intellectuals, artists, and managers who had criticized the CCP. These people were requested by the CCP to speak out regarding the CCP's performance since the revolution. They were told that their suggestions were needed to improve the revolution, however, once they did speak out with their suggestions on how to improve the government the CCP had them arrested and jailed without due process. This action caused the CCP to lose much of its credibility with the people.

The Great Leap Forward: 1958–1960

It was Mao's belief that under a command economy the central leadership could determine the economic policies and the allocation of resources for the whole country. One of the purposes of this was to unite China as one country with one goal: to industrialize the countryside. Mao thought he could accomplish this by forcing people to relocate into very large communes, economic and administrative units consisting of between 30,000 to 70,000 peasants. Mao sent young urban intellectuals to the countryside to teach the farmers while learning about agriculture from the farmers. This was called being "sent-down" (Dreyer 1996). He wanted all these mobilized masses in the countryside to farm, raise livestock, and build "backyard furnaces" for smelting steel. Mao's goal was to exceed England's steel production in 15 years (Dreyer 1996). The majority of the people being "relocated" from the cities to the communes had no prior knowledge or experience in hard physical labor, farming, or smelting steel. Virtually therefore everything they built was useless. The concept of communes did not go over well with the farmers either; many of them set their fields on fire and killed all their livestock rather than give them over to the state (Dreyer 1996).

Another demand by the CCP, and one that went too far, was that everyone in the commune had to eat together in a big hall. This last demand caused the peasants to revolt and to refuse to work, because it directly interfered with their personal quiet family time. To the Chinese people there is nothing more important than family, especially in times of uncertainly and change (Christiansen 1996).

The Great Leap Forward was a complete failure and Mao lost power within the CCP. This was the spark that ignited a very bloody intraleadership conflict called the Cultural Revolution (Joffe 1975).

Cultural Revolution: 1966–1976

The Cultural Revolution spanned more than 10 years. Many terrible things happened during this period, including the deaths of tens of millions of people. The purpose of the Cultural Revolution was to "mobilize the masses without restraint" so they could have the opportunity to "educate themselves." The CCP promoted this by attacking the "Four Olds": old ideas, old customs, old culture, and old habits.

There was also the politicization of education and cultural production as a means of "thought reform." This was essential because politicization was brought about due to an increase of expertise outside the CCP, i.e., teachers, professionals, managers, and government leaders. These outside experts were considered harmful to Chinese culture because they had "revisionist" tendencies in social and political life (Christiansen 1996).

In reality, the Cultural Revolution was an attack by Mao on all who had opposed him or his thought. It re-established Mao as the person in complete control of the CCP and all of China. After the Great Leap Forward failed, Mao lost considerable *mianzi* and the Cultural Revolution was his way of doing away with all who had opposed him (Joffe 1975).

Major events included the Little Red Book, the Red Guards, and the redistribution of people. The Little Red Book was a collection of Mao's quotations that was published in a little diary size book with a plastic red cover. Small enough to carry everywhere, it was waved as a sign of support, and was necessary for showing support for Mao. The next major event that took place was when Mao called out the Red Guards in August 1966. The Red Guard was a large group of young adults that spread out all over China to enforce revolutionary purity by attacking the Old Four: old ideas, culture, habits, and customs. The Red Guards turned on all those whom they thought were power-holders, including their parents, teachers, police, public officials, and the CCP. In time, they turned on people within the Red Guard itself.

During this time, every step that every person took was watched; each building had a party official in it monitoring everything everyone did, 24 hours a day. There was no privacy; if it was not the monitor in the building, it was the Red Guards, or someone within a work-unit who was watching. The Chinese people during this period were prisoners within their own country. They were hounded with one propaganda campaign after another; they could trust no one, except family members and even this was uncertain at times, because the Red Guards would even turn on their own parents.

The result that is remembered by the Chinese people is that almost everything they held dear was ripped from their lives: friends, money, careers, and homes. Due to the total confusion, economic production, for the most part, stopped because the bosses were sent to "re-education" camps by the Red Guards as power-holders, as were the replacing bosses. This continual influx into the countryside of "political criminals" who were being "sent-down" by the Red Guards for "re-education" was a disaster in the making. Most of these "political criminals" knew nothing about farming, which resulted in crops not being planted on time, and a food shortage (Christiansen 1996). These were not isolated cases, it is estimated that 10 percent of the Chinese population or about 100 million people (that is over one third of the population of the United States) were targets of the Cultural Revolution. In addition, it is estimated that tens of thousands of people lost their lives during this ten-year span (Ogden 1993). The Cultural Revolution was a catastrophic event in China that negatively affected everyone's life.

Calling it a complete failure does not begin to adequately describe this event, which continued until Mao died on September 9, 1976. One of the worst victims was the CCP itself because of the attacks on many of its leaders and because of a breakdown of both traditional Chinese morality and Marxist-Leninist values. In the end, the people lost faith in and respect for the CCP, a feeling that is still held by the masses today (Ogden 1993).

The June forth incident (Also known as 6-4): June 4, 1989

This is the name given to the violent crackdown by the CCP on intellectuals, professors, and students that occurred on June 4th, 1989. The protesters were participating in a peaceful protest against the government's lack of action regarding the deteriorating living conditions created by fixed incomes that were being eroded away by inflation. As the protesters grew in number, and the number of protesters grew in strength, and intensity, the grievances also grew to include charges of corruption and calls for democracy, which the CCP could not accept. The students were also gaining sympathetic support from the public and among the more open-minded members of the CCP and Politburo. In addition, the CCP was also feeling pressure to resolve the student demonstrations very quickly because of a visit by Gorbachev, the Soviet leader that was planned on May 12. The CCP was rapidly losing its options to resolve this situation without losing *mianzi* or adding validity to the students' protests. In an attempt to resolve the situation, Premier Li Peng had a televised meeting with the students that only drew added support to the students when one of them fainted on television. The response of the CCP to these events was to declare a state of emergency for Beijing on June 2. Then on June 4, the PLA was ordered by the Politburo to march into the square and to clear it. The

PLA opened fire on the students and it is estimated that between 100 and 1,000 protesters were killed (Christiansen 1996).

This incident concluded on June 4th, but the demonstrations had gone on for months before the crackdown. News of the students' protests spread out to other cities and to the countryside via Chinese television and radio programs. This only caused more students to go to Beijing to join in the protest with their own agendas and ideas of what needs to be addressed. These actions caused additional small-scale protests throughout China, which included a month-long walkout by the students and teachers at most of the universities.

When one group of students negotiated with the government, another group would soon arrive to demand additional concessions. This created a process that was never-ending because the students' lists of demands kept getting longer. There were a few student leaders who tried to work with the CCP to resolve the situation, and this caused the students to split into various political camps, each with its own agenda (Christiansen 1996, Chinoy 1997).

The student situation caused the members of the CCP's Politburo to start their own intraleadership fighting again over how to handle the students. The hard-liners, with the support of Deng, were able to "send down" supporters of the students within the Politburo and replace them with additional hard-liners. This single action set the reform movement back ten to fifteen years. This gave the hard-liners the votes they needed, with Deng's support, to have the PLA end the student protests. These actions sent a clear message to everyone: to the students, to the Chinese people, and to the world; China may be opening up its markets, but the CCP is still in charge (Dreyer 1996).

An interesting note about the crackdown is that throughout this demonstration there were troops in the Square keeping order. The students had actually established friendly relationships with these soldiers, sharing their food and water with them. When the first order came to clear the Square, these troops refused. The CCP had to bring troops in from outside provinces to clear the Square.

Jiang Zemin, Announced as the Party General Secretary: June 1989

After the June Forth incident, there was a strong backlash from the world community and from the Chinese people, causing the hard-liners to lose support within the CCP and the Politburo. Deng, in an attempt to bring calm to the CCP, appointed Jiang Zemin to be his successor.

It has been suggested that Deng ordered the clearing of the Square because the hard-liners were gaining power due to the students' protests. It has also been suggested that by ordering the clearing of the Square, Deng was trying to prevent the hard-liner Li Ping from becoming Party leader. Li Ping's appointment as Party leader would have reversed China's economic and political growth. Deng was able to avoid this by allowing the hard-liners to gain control of the Politburo during the protests. This allowed them to be the ones to give the order to clear the Square, which caused them to lose support. This power shift was enough to allow Deng to appoint Jiang as Party leader, which then shifted the Politburo back to a more moderate approach (Dreyer 1996).

Jiang removes People's Liberation Army influence from top party seats: 1989

During the 15th National Congress, Jiang Zemin, China's President and Communist Party Chief, was able to remove a few people from the 192-member Central Committee. One of the men removed was 72 year old Qiao Shi, the National People's Congress chairman and the CCP's No. 3 official. Qiao resigned completely rather than take a demotion (China's Party leaders nod and wink at Marx. International Herald Tribune, September 19, 1997: 4).

Others removed included Liu Huaqing, a Politburo member and the only military man on the seven-man standing committee. This has also been seen as a major setback to the PLA, because now it does not have a representative on the Politburo. Now that the PLA has no representation in the political arena, Jiang is free to handpick his top generals. This deliberate reorganization of the Politburo could only mean that there were changes coming to the PLA (China shake-up strengthens Jiang: Removal of No.3 officials seen as setback for reformers. International Herald Tribune, September 19, 1997: 1).

Jiang also removed Hu Ping, son-in-law of Deng Xiaoping. Deng was the person who appointed Jiang to his current post as Party leader. Hu Ping was the head of the Poly Group, which was active in arms dealing, the military, and other areas of interest. Other people close to those two also lost their seats within the Central Committee, thus eliminating much of their *guanxi* within the CCP.

Jiang tells the People's Liberation Army to sell off its 20,000 businesses: 1999

Jiang told the PLA to sell off its 20,000 enterprises and focus on becoming a professional military. That is an order that will probably be obeyed because Jiang has replaced the top generals with ones he has handpicked.

Analysis of How the Political Events Reinforce the Four Cultural Complexes

These political events have illustrated how the CCP abused its power and the trust of the people by targeting over 100 million people for punishment for political, economic, and social reasons. These people were sent to prisons and re-education camps, or they just disappeared. These actions were taken to ensure that the CCP and Mao's authority were not questioned by anybody, not even high-ranking CCP officials. To accomplish this, they completely abandoned the entire legal system. Their actions included the suspension of the constitution as well as the arrest of almost everyone connected with the legal system. These events, combined with countless others, have caused recent generations to develop a fear and mistrust of most authority figures and institutions, which in turn has reinforced the four cultural complexes.

Often in these kinds of situations, fear and mistrust of a government are expressed by the people in the form of literature and art. For years, the CCP and the NPC have tried to keep the people's voices regarding their history of abuse silent. Even as positive changes occur within China and the doors to China's economy open and as the hard-liners of China's communist system are replaced with more moderate policy makers the people are expressing their frustration with the CCP and the NPC's policies in the form of literature and art.

The following are a few poems reflecting either the political events or the situations that were occurring at that time. In 1979, immediately after the Cultural Revolution, Su Ming wrote: "Another political upheaval has convulsed China. The Gang of Four has been rehabilitated...If you look at the history of China and the weakness of her political institutions; this is not so totally improbable" (Barme 1989: 119). Another poem was published in the Hong Kong Express on April 4, 1986, which discusses how fear of the government still stalks the land.

The feudal age of the first Great Emperor has gone, never to return. But the 'spectre from within the ancient fortress' still prowls our land. The specter of Party rule (rather than democracy), of rule by the individual (rather than rule of law), of power (rather than right), still stalks the land. The fate of the leaders of the Chinese Democracy Movement, the regime's opposition to liberalization, the staunch upholding of the Four Principles, are all manifestations of this Specter (Barme 1989: 120).

Sun Jingxuan is another poet who has chosen to speak-out against the CCP and the NPC through publishing the poem "A Specter Prowls Our Land." Sun was also punished for this poem and later published a self-examination paper called "A Serious flawed work: Sun Jingxuan's Self-criticism, which criticized his previous poem. The following is an excerpt from the original poem discussing this fear of governmental and/or the CCP's authority:

> "Brothers have you seen the specter prowling our land? In this century, this Nuclear Age, to talk of specters seems absurd but it's the truth—the terrible and tragic truth! The specter, like a gust of wind, like a wisp of smoke, prowls unencumbered o'er our land; trails like a shadow, clutches with invisible claws, silently sucks blood and marrow, dictates every action, controls every thought; tramples on dignity, destroys the quest for beauty, the yearning for love. The slightest hint and you are locked away for years in some dark and gloomy prison cell! This specter decrees death, posthumous humiliation, or tolerates lives of vexatious vegetation; you are, then, spectral slave and spectral subject, without the right to cry out in protest" (Barme 1989: 121–122).

And further in the poem, Sun wrote:

"The decaying palaces, the dark temples crumbled, crumbled, crashed to the ground and the red flag waved in the bright skies of China; like children we wept tears of joy, forgot the hardships and sorrows of the past. But how brief were the days of cheer! Reality came, dragging with it bitter disenchantment: we had thought ourselves masters of our fate, that we could now live happy and free on our land, but now we found ourselves mere "screws" driven tight into some machine; numbers on a statistical chart, Pieces on a Go Board–black and white. Flesh and blood and thinking mind we had but could not wreak feeling, well or thought, oh misery! We were abstractions! Our bounden duty to raise our hands and clap.... After all, a revolution is no stroll down the street. A cleansing tide is bound to damage ships and homes. Perhaps this childish goodwill lies at the root of our misfortune.... But even we are human, even we can think, and in the end we saw: Our sweat and blood, given for the Great Edifice of Socialism, and built a cathedral of fear..." (Barme 1989: 125–126).

These poems are a reflection of the current mistrust and fear that the Chinese people feel towards the CCP, the government, and authority in general. This is not to say that everything the CCP does is wrong, because that is not the case. If it were the case, there would have been another revolution already. The point being made here is that, over the centuries, the Chinese developed a culturally defined defense mechanism (the four complexes) against a government and authority figures they could not trust. The purpose of discussing these recent political events is to illustrate how they have impressed fear and mistrust of the government and of authority figures into the personalities of individuals, thus reinforcing the four cultural complexes.

How the CCP Utilized the Four Cultural Complexes to Control China

When the Great Leap was brought to an end by the Politburo, Mao lost *mianzi*. The only way Mao could restore his *mianzi* was through an act of revenge that would cause the people who were his political opponents to lose *mianzi*. The political and economic situations in the years that followed the Great Leap were much better, compared to the years during the Great Leap. These were also years of plotting, planning and maneuvering by Mao to restore his *mianzi*. Mao's time came when his greatest opponent, P'eng Ten-huai wrote a letter of opinion regarding Mao and his right to lead. With this letter, P'eng Ten-huai not only questioned Mao's ability to lead, but also his right to lead, thus causing Mao to lose even more *mianzi*. For Mao, this was his time to act and he did. Through his *guanxi*, Mao was able to defend against this attempt to remove him from power. Mao was also able to have P'eng Ten-huai and his followers removed from the Politburo. Then, a short time later, P'eng Ten-huai died in a plane

crash, reportedly on his way to Moscow. This paved
the way for the start of the Cultural Revolution, during which time Mao ruled the PRC with an iron
hand. Once Mao returned to power, he was able to
utilize the four cultural complexes (*mianzi*, *keqi*,
guanxi, and *renqing*) to pressure his friends to follow
him and his policies. Once he had their commitment
he took his revenge on everyone who ever opposed
him or disagreed with his policies. Mao ruled for ten
years with an iron hand, and sent the Red Guards
out to enforce his policies. Then, just as suddenly as
the Cultural Revolution started, it ended with Mao's
death. It ended because others within the CCP understood that Mao's policies were not working and
that the country was in economic and political ruins.
Therefore when Mao died, these followers did not
feel obligated to fulfill any more *renqing* toward Mao.

With this sudden end of the Cultural Revolution
came a power vacuum and a power struggle was
started by the "Gang of Four," which was led by
Mao's wife. The members of the "Gang of Four" were
all major players in the Cultural Revolution. The
power struggle quickly ended when the "Gang of
Four", including Mao's wife were arrested. Then
much later, they were tried for crimes against the
people. In the end, it was Deng Xiaoping who was
able to gain enough *guanxi* to win the power struggle.

Once in power, Deng was not challenged. One of
the first things Deng did was to replace Mao's supporters with people who had well-established *guanxi*.
This extended his power to a position where it was
uncontested. Deng was not able to accomplish all of
this due to overwhelming support for his ideas or

policies, but because everyone was still too afraid and tired from the political bloodbath that had persisted for the past ten years during the Cultural Revolution. Through his reforms and through his ability to place supporters in almost every essential political and governmental position, Deng was able to implement one of his most noted policies, which was to decentralize the power base by spreading the power over several people. Deng's purpose was to decentralize political power to prevent one person, including himself from having too much power. He understood, from a victim's point of view, that one person with all the power only leads to abuse of that power. By implementing these policies and placing his supporters in essential areas, Deng was able to calm the political infighting.

Another change Deng was able to implement was a new constitution, which focused on re-developing a legal system based on written laws. These reforms brought over ten years of economic prosperity to China, giving it one of the largest economies in the world and giving it global player status in the world economy.

By spreading the power base out over more people, Deng ensured that events that occurred during the Cultural Revolution would not happen again. At the same time, Deng lost some political battles, including the student protests in 1989 when he ordered the PLA to clear the Square on June 4, 1989.

It has been suggested, by Mike Chinoy (1997) in his book *China Live,* that the clearing of the Square was one way that Deng was able to manipulate the situation back in favor of the moderates. The result was a backlash against the hard-liners in the Politburo, and against their *guanxi* network. This allowed the reappointment of moderates throughout the CCP, including allowing Deng to appoint Jiang Zemin, a moderate and former mayor of Shanghai as the Party General Secretary.

A short time later Deng died. His death did trigger another intraleadership power struggle. Because he had spread the power base among several important officials thus weakening the influence of their *guanxi* networks, the transition of power was easier than when Mao died.

The Relationship between the Chinese Communist Party and The National People's Congress

Since 1949, China has been united under the Communist system forged by Mao Zedong.

The relationship between the CCP and the State is of concern to a Cultural Translator because understanding how they are organized in relation to each other will provide insight into the interpretation of political events. The political arena in China is complex and often filled with intraleadership conflict. Understanding this complexity requires an examination of the structure of the CCP, the National People's Congress (NPC), the PLA, and the legal system in the PRC.

The political and government organizations in China have a unique relationship. The CCP is the head of the PRC, and its will is supreme. The CCP's purpose is to provide spiritual and ideological input for policies, while the State's purpose is to execute the policies provided by the CCP by working out the administrative details and supervising the routine decisions that follow (Dreyer 1996). To ensure that the CCP's will is done, the military falls under direct control of the CCP, not the State. Mao defined the role of the military when he said, "the party must always control the gun, the gun must never control the party" (Dreyer 1996: 189). He established that the CCP and not the State will lead the country and that everything will serve the will of the CCP. This was an important part of Mao's plan because he strongly believed in the concept of a permanent revolution, which meant the continuous disruption of settled routines to prevent the evils of the old society from re-emerging. To accomplish this Mao needed the army to enforce the CCP's ideology.

To ensure that the ideology of the CCP was unquestioned, the Party also decreed that only it would appoint or elect people to the top offices within the PLA and the State. These appointments were filled by the same top CCP leaders who had decided the will of the CCP in the first place thus ensuring that their will be done. They wore two hats, one as the top ideology-setting leaders of the CCP and another as the top officials in the PLA or the State doing the CCP's dictates. This ensured that the will of the CCP was carried out exactly as the CCP intended; the role of the PLA was to ensure that no one had any other ideas.

Since the founding of the CCP, the PLA has had a voice in the decision making process through members on the Politburo and the Standing Committee of the CCP. In 1998, however, Jiang Zemin removed all PLA-appointed members from the Politburo and the Standing Committee of the CCP. This was the first time that the PLA did not have an independent voice in the CCP. This dramatic event could only mean that there are changes coming to the PLA in the near future.

To illustrate how the CCP controls the National People's Congress (NPC) and the PLA, there are organizational flow charts of the Chinese Communist Party, the government of the People's Republic of China, and the People's Liberation Army located at the end of the chapter. These flow charts show where and how the CCP exercises its will over the State and the PLA. They also show that the PLA consists of CCP and state personnel, and that it is the Central Military Commission, on the state side, that administers the PLA.

These flow charts also illustrate how much overlap there is between the CCP and the State. It is clear that the CCP can and does exercise its control over the state to ensure that its will be done. The CCP flowchart also illustrates that only a very small group actually sets the ideology for the entire country. This method of leading, coupled with the Chinese reliance on *guanxi* really means that only a handful of people actually run the CCP, the State, and the PLA. During the 1980s under Deng, the power base did widen somewhat to encompass more people, and Jiang has continued this trend. However, the people to whom they are giving the power are people with whom they have well established *guanxi*.

The result of such a centralization power can be seen in political events. A good example is the power struggle that occurred after the collapse of the Great Leap Forward. Its breakdown set off the disputes that defined intraleadership relations in the first half the 1960s, thus linking the collapse of the Great Leap Forward with the Cultural Revolution.

The Great Leap and the Cultural Revolution are linked because certain top CCP officials and their supporters (through *guanxi*) took sides against Mao, the central power holder. The Great Leap was Mao's idea and so were the policies that he proposed to the CCP for approval. Most of the CCP originally agreed with Mao for various personal reasons, but many changed their minds and spoke out against it when they actually saw its shortcomings and realized that their personal expectations were not going to be met. This, together with the failure of the "Hundred Flowers Campaign", resulted in Mao relinquishing his ceremonial post as Chairman of the Republic during the Wuhan conference in December 1958. Mao considered this a personal attack on his abilities and a loss of face. He plotted his revenge and climbed back to power between 1958 and 1966, and then in 1966, he started the Cultural Revolution (Joffe 1975).

At the Central Committee Lushan conference held in July and August 1959 to discuss the policies of the Great Leap, a power struggle erupted. The one leading the attack on the policies of the Great Leap was P'eng Teh-huai, who at the time was the Minister of Defense and a member of the Politburo. P'eng and his supporters were denounced at Lushan and dismissed from their posts, but their views were shared by other CCP members. P'eng and his supporters were proven right in time and their predictions became reality.

The reason why this power struggle was different was that P'eng wrote a "Letter of Opinion" to

Mao and distributed it to his colleagues at the conference. This letter attacked the Great Leap's policies and told how they brought about more damage
than benefits. P'eng's actions were a violation of *keqi*
and caused Mao to lose *mianzi*. Though the Great
Leap Forward was causing Mao to lose support within the Party and most of the major players within
the Party agreed with P'eng, P'eng and his supporters were removed from their posts. It was this single
action by P'eng, which formed the major theme underlying the process that propelled Mao and the
Chinese leadership to the Cultural Revolution (Joffe
1975).

The conflict between the Mao and P'eng continued over the years and erupted again over a difference of opinion regarding Soviet aid to develop China's nuclear capabilities. Mao and his supporters believed that the demands by the Soviets in exchange
for this aid were too high and compromised China's
independence and integrity. P'eng, on the other
hand, was willing to consider the terms demanded by
the Soviets if it meant modernizing the army and
developing nuclear capabilities. P'eng's attitude was
one of temporary reliance on the Soviets that would
gain China sophisticated weaponry and a conven-
tional strategy. Mao believed that this left China
depending too heavily on the Soviets. He did not
want to put too much faith in sophisticated weapons;
he was relying on the "human element" and the doctrine of a "people's war" (Joffe 1975). It was this difference of opinions that threw China into its worst
crisis since the revolution (Joffe 1875; Dreyer 1996).

The intraleadership fighting within the CCP continued, but Mao regained support and a strong dom-

inant position, because the power struggle was starting to question Mao's personal ability and right to lead. When Mao's right to lead was questioned, his supporters stood by his side because, while they may have questioned his policies and seen the Great Leap as a giant mistake, they never questioned his right to lead. Thus, Mao launched his revenge on all of those who opposed his ideology and his policies that focused on the disruption of patterned behavior; he started the Cultural Revolution.

During the ten years of the Cultural Revolution, his opponents were killed or were sent to "re-education" camps in the countryside, or they just disappeared. The constitution was suspended, and the legal system was completely abandoned. Millions of people all over China were victims to the Red Guard, including top people within the CCP. There were no rules, and no organization. There was no control system that was not questioned by Mao and the Red Guards. This absolute power wielded by the Red Guards ended conclusively any type of power struggle and established Mao as the sole head of the CCP (Christiansen 1996; Dreyer 1996).

The Cultural Revolution turned out to be the darkest spot in recent Chinese history because a small group wielded absolute power through the manipulation of the four cultural complexes of *mianzi*, *keqi*, *guanxi*, and *renqing*. By manipulating these cultural complexes, they were able to control all of China with an iron hand. If anyone or anything, including the legal system, opposed their will, they used the cultural complexes to destroy it.

This is the true power of cultural knowledge and it makes the point of this book. The cultural mindset and the cultural complexes that both support and reflect it are very real. It is the Cultural Translator's job to understand them. Once the Cultural Translator has a working understanding of the cultural mindset and the cultural complexes, he/she can turn this information into a strategic advantage for his/her company, an advantage that can be utilized during business negotiations as well as in ongoing business ventures.

Figure 3.2

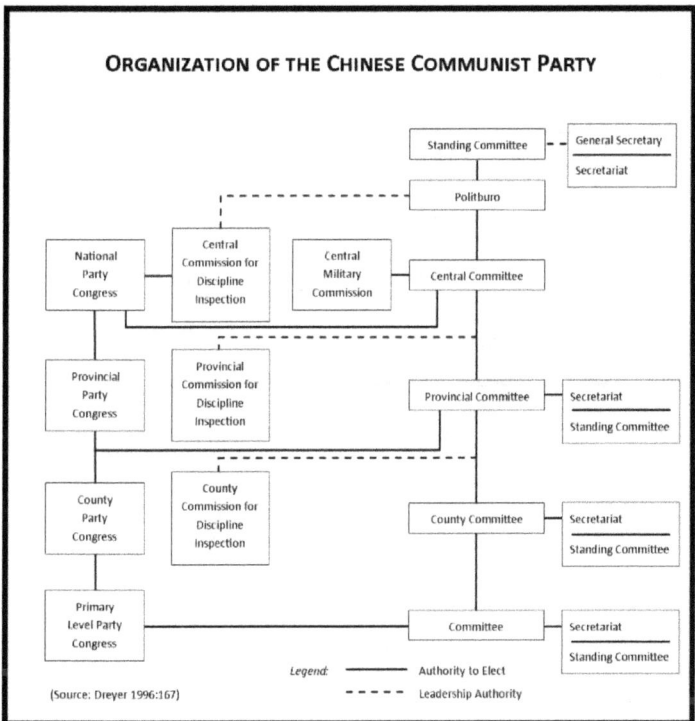

ORGANIZATION OF THE CHINESE COMMUNIST PARTY

(Source: Dreyer 1996:167)

Legend:
——— Authority to Elect
- - - - Leadership Authority

Figure 3.3

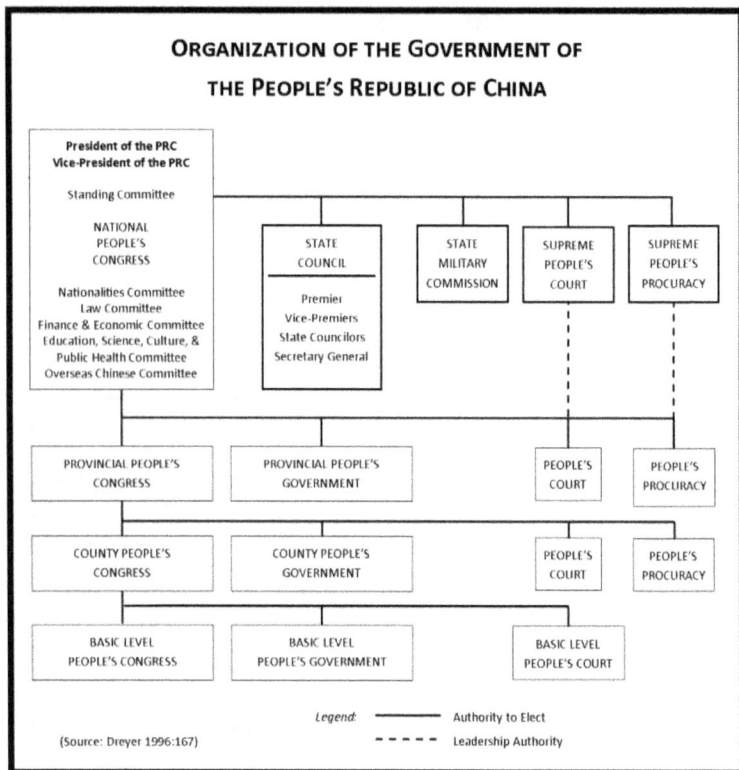

ORGANIZATION OF THE GOVERNMENT OF THE PEOPLE'S REPUBLIC OF CHINA

President of the PRC
Vice-President of the PRC

Standing Committee

NATIONAL PEOPLE'S CONGRESS

Nationalities Committee
Law Committee
Finance & Economic Committee
Education, Science, Culture, &
Public Health Committee
Overseas Chinese Committee

STATE COUNCIL

Premier
Vice-Premiers
State Councilors
Secretary General

STATE MILITARY COMMISSION

SUPREME PEOPLE'S COURT

SUPREME PEOPLE'S PROCURACY

PROVINCIAL PEOPLE'S CONGRESS

PROVINCIAL PEOPLE'S GOVERNMENT

PEOPLE'S COURT

PEOPLE'S PROCURACY

COUNTY PEOPLE'S CONGRESS

COUNTY PEOPLE'S GOVERNMENT

PEOPLE'S COURT

PEOPLE'S PROCURACY

BASIC LEVEL PEOPLE'S CONGRESS

BASIC LEVEL PEOPLE'S GOVERNMENT

BASIC LEVEL PEOPLE'S COURT

Legend:
——— Authority to Elect
- - - - Leadership Authority

(Source: Dreyer 1996:167)

Figure 3.4

MILITARY SYSTEM OF THE PEOPLE'S REPUBLIC OF CHINA

Central Military Commission (Party)		Central Military Commission (State)
	Ministry of National Defense of the State Council	

People's Liberation Army

General Logistics Department	General Political Department	General Staff Department

Service Arms

Air Force	Second Artillery	Navy	People's Armed Police

East Sea Fleet	North Sea Fleet	North Sea Fleet

Military Regions

Beijing	Chengdu	Guangzhou	Jinan	Lanzhou	Nanjing	Shenyang

Military | Districts

Hebei	Guizhou	Guangdong	Henan	Gansu	Anhui	Heilongjiang
Inner Mongolia	Sichuan	Guangxi	Shandong	Ningxia	Fujian	Jilin
Shanxi	Tibet	Hainan		Qinghai	Jiangsu	Liaoning
	Yunnan	Hubei		Shaanxi	Jiangxi	
		Hunan		Xinjiang	Zhejiang	
				Nanjiang		

(Source: Dreyer 1996:167)

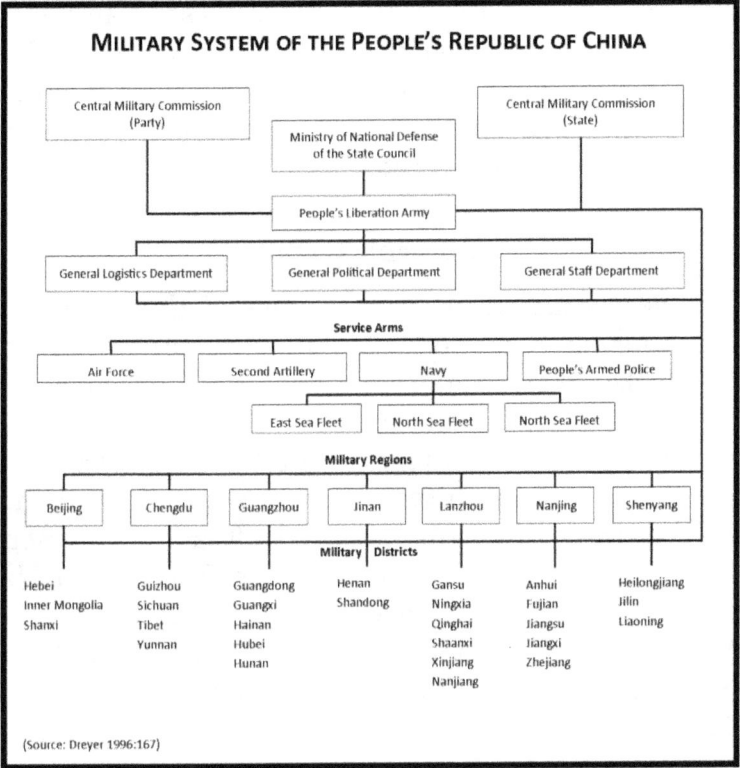

The Legal System

The purpose of a legal system is to create a sense of fairness and a place to seek redress of wrongs. In the arena of international business, the legal system establishes the "rules of the game". As such, it is an important factor in doing business because it should create a "fair" playing field for the players by allowing companies to examine the laws and understand the rules prior to investing.

In addition to knowing these laws however, an understanding of the socio-cultural system in which they function is also critical, because the laws define the specific "rules of the game," whereas the socio-cultural system establishes the framework in which the laws are administered.

Specific Laws

The specific laws or the "rules of the game" for investing exist on two levels, the national and the local levels. The legal issues regarding specific "national" laws governing how to invest and the requirements for investment are addressed by the international community, through trade agreements such as the North American Free Trade Agreement (NAFTA), the Association of South East Asian Nations (ASEAN), and the World Trade Organizations (WTO), as well as many others. Additionally, there are various governmental institutions, such as local Consulate General Offices and the U.S. Department of Commerce that will assist companies in importing or exporting their goods. In addition, private and not-for-profit organizations, as well as an increasing number of attorneys who specialize in international law, can assist companies with many import and export problems, such as letters of credit, regulations regarding the products' origins, or what forms need to be filled out.

In addition, foreign companies have found their own ways around the uncertainty created by the national and local laws and procedures by establishing various types of joint ventures and independent distributors. These approaches allow time for an investing company to gain much needed confidence in the foreign market and government, as well as time to develop *guanxi*.

Since Deng opened the economic doors to China, the number of equity joint ventures created rose from 63 in 1979/81 to 7,859 in 1991. Throughout this time period there were 24,119 equity joint ventures established, with a total of $20,904,300,000 in capital investment. The number of contractual joint ventures during the same time period increased from 683 to 1,731 a year to a total of 11,042. These are the true indicators that foreign companies are growing in their confidence in the Chinese political arena and legal system. That confidence can also be seen in the huge rise of wholly-foreign-owned companies in China. During the same period, these increased from 25 to 2,696. This steady increase of capital moving into the PRC not only demonstrates an increase in investors' confidence in the PRC, it also demonstrates that, at the national level, China is serious about attracting capital investment (De Keijzer 1995).

Conditions at the local level, however, are more difficult to anticipate and cope with, because "the State rules but it does not actually control" (Macarthney 1995, Reuter, transmitted 95-03-17 at 19:39:01 EST). Cultural Translators need, therefore, to focus on the local situation, both because the laws at the local level are changing and because it is the local enforcement of both the national and local laws that ultimately matters. The biggest problems with local authorities are corruption and fees, hidden costs, and taxes that are assigned to companies. Corruption is a problem in China, sometimes because there is a fine line between corruption and *guanxi*; in many cases however it is clearly corruption. Many additional fees assigned, however, are not bribes. Most of these fees are assigned at the end of the year when government officials realize they overspent for the year and need to make-up the difference. These fees are assigned without notice generally to companies that can afford them, and they are made retroactive for the entire year (Macarthney 1995).

Corruption

Corruption is endemic and is part of the cost of doing business in China. The problem is compounded by the foreign entrepreneur not knowing, first, how many people would need to receive a bribe in order for the bribe to be effective, and, second, who does not need to receive a bribe. It can be extremely difficult to find out who actually makes the decisions under the Chinese Communist system.

Corruption is an integral part of life in China's new market-driven socialist system. The use of *guanxi* is no longer just used to keep family and friends out of trouble; it is now being exploited more than ever to make a few people very rich. Although the Chinese government has created anti-corruption programs such as the TIPS program (discussed in the next section), corruption remains an integral part of how things get done in China. The corruption that exists in China today is no longer limited to the lower levels of local governments; it reaches as high as the Politburo.

The CCP is fully aware of the extent and seriousness of the amount of corruption in China. In an interview with Chinese Premier Zhu Rongji that was published online at *Asiaweek.com*, Premier Zhu addressed the corruption problem.

Asiaweek asked: "Isn't it time to take anti-corruption campaigns away from the party and the government, and hand them to independent commissions?"

Premier Zhu answered: "It's not a matter of commissions or no commission doing the job. In the end, it comes down to building the rule of law and the socialist legal system. The views of the government on corruption are clear. And although I must admit that our laws need improvement, the rampant corruption is not a problem of a lack of law, but a problem of implementation. There are 180,000 judges in China, but only 10% have received university education. So many are not up to their task. China has similar education problems with its police force. Progress in the fight against corruption will be in tandem with advances in building the legal system".

Premier Zhu's answer not only acknowledges that there is a problem with corruption in China, it is also acknowledges that it is rampant. To demonstrate the CCP commitment to eliminating corruption among public and CCP officials, the CCP has cracked down and publicized the arrests of top local CCP and governmental officials. They have also implemented a program, called "TIPS," to generate leads in finding corrupt officials. The following are four cases of corruption that have been widely publicized: Xie Jianbang was the Vice-mayor of Ningbo; Zhang Kaike was the former secretary of the Qijiang County Committee for the CPC; Wang Baosen was the Deputy Mayor of Beijing, and Cheng Kejie was the Vice Chairman of the Standing Committee of the National People's Congress.

Xie Jianbang was recently sentenced to death after accepting bribes for business favors. Xie Jianbang, the Vice-mayor of Ningbo, a city in east China's Zhenjiang Province, was deprived of political rights for life, expelled from the CCP for life, and had property worth 100,000 Yuan confiscated by the Intermediate People's Court in Huzhou, in Zhejiang. He was found guilty of accepting 315,000 Yuan, HK$120,000, and US$25,000 in bribes to assist general managers of some local companies and investors from Hong Kong, between 1993 and 1998. He was the vice-mayor of Ningbo and a member of the standing committee of the municipal CCP committee; he was also director of the Administration Committee of the Ningbo Economic and Technical Development Zone from November 1992 to August 1995 ("Vice-mayor punished for receiving bribes," China Daily June 14, 1999:3)

Zhang Kaike, a former secretary of the Qijiang County Committee for the Communist Party of China, will soon go to the Chongqing's No. 1 Intermediate Court. He will face charges by the procurator officials of taking 342,000 Yuan in bribes and of dereliction of duty relating to his involvement in a bridge collapse that occurred on January 4, 1999.

The 4 bridges collapsed killing 40 people, seriously injuring 14 more, and causing 6 million Yuan in monetary losses ('Silicon Valley' takes shape: Zhongguancun to focus on the development of high-tech sector. China Daily, June 22, 1997: 3).

Wang Baosen was the Beijing Deputy Mayor who committed suicide last year after being charged with embezzlement. According to the Beijing prosecutor, He Fangba, there have been 18 people charged and 7 more are under investigation. He Fangba would not comment on whether deposed Beijing Communist Party Chief, Chen Xitong was also under investigation.

Chen Xitong and Jiang Zemin were both candidates for the position of President and Communist Party Leader in Deng's later years. It was Jiang who Deng picked as his successor. Chen Xitong was known to be bitter about this and he claimed that Jiang cheated him (Mufson 1997e). Chen ruled over the capital Beijing for 12 years as mayor and then as party chief; he was on the CCP's Politburo. This made him the highest man in the CCP history to be investigated for wrongdoing. *Guanxi* is already working to bring on the spin-doctors: Beijing Mayor Li Qiyan in the Beijing Daily referred only to "errors" committed by Chen while underlining the "crimes" committed by Wang (AFP 1996: 18 to be charged in Beijing for $3 billion corruption scandal).

Cheng Kejie was executed on Thursday, September 14, 2000 for taking bribes worth $5 million. Cheng was the vice chairman of the Standing Committee of the National People's Congress, thus making him the highest ranking CCP official to be tried, convicted, and executed in the 50 years of Communist rule.

The Tips Program

As the execution of Cheng Kejie has illustrated, the CCP is clamping down on corruption even at the highest levels. In fighting corruption, the Supreme People's Procuratorate (SPP) announced that the last week of every June will be a week of nationwide publicity on tips. "Tips" refers to information from people who inform the government about public officials who are involved in corruption. Such tips generate about 80 percent of the cases handled by the prosecutor's offices. A further indication that the Supreme People's Procuratorate is serious about reducing corruption is that it sent out tens of thousands of procurators from more than 3,600 procurator's offices across the country to offer consultations on tips and other legal affairs to ordinary Chinese people. There is even a special day every month when tipsters can meet with the procurator-general or one of the vice-procurators-general, personally. The SPP has also established a hotline number that ends in "2000" where people can call in with their tips (Meng 1999).

Clearly, as Premier Zhu pointed out, corruption is a problem in China, but one that is being addressed by the CCP. It is not the only problem facing investors in China, however. Another major problem are the fees charged to companies, including State Owned Enterprises (SOEs) and other private enterprises that the local authorities think can afford to pay them.

Many additional fees, however, are not bribes. Most of these fees are assigned at the end of the year when government officials realize they overspent for the year and need to make-up the difference. These fees are assigned without notice, generally to companies that can afford them, and they are made retroactive for the entire year (Macarthney, Jane. Risks high in China business). These fees are not bribes, however many of these fees are unauthorized by the national government.

A Case Study: McDonalds

The mayor of Beijing, Jia Qinglin, conducted a study to find out what has slowed the economic investment into Beijing. He ordered a report focusing on McDonald's to find out why foreign investment in Beijing has stagnated. McDonald's was chosen because it owns 38 restaurants in Beijing. The report found that there were an additional 31 unauthorized fees charged to McDonald's, in addition to their taxes, to pay for family planning, flowers for the city streets, and a propaganda campaign telling the Chinese to be more gracious. These additional illegal fees were costing McDonald's thousands of dollars a year.

These were unauthorized fees put in place by local governmental agencies that needed to raise additional revenue to compensate for shortfalls due to budget cuts. Such additional fees are common, according to foreign investors. Even the SOEs are assigned fees that cost them millions of dollars a year.

The State is trying to end this problem by calling on local officials to stop the collection of these unauthorized fees, especially from SOEs.

In McDonald's case, out of the 31 fees, only 2 were clearly justified. Another eight were questionable, and 17 were clearly illegitimate. The report did not address the other four. These additional fees were: $4.30 per parking space charged for traffic safety; $1.20 an employee charged for public tree-planting; and thousands of dollars assessed for river dredging (Beijing has only one small river). Additionally, each outlet paid $300 to $600 a year for "spiritual civilization." This was to put up banners to tell people to be more cultured. This was President Jiang Zemin's campaign, and was probably one of the two fees judged to be clearly justified.

Other fees included increases in trash fees from $600 a year to $1200. When a health inspector found three flies in a kitchen, the restaurant was charged $3,600 (it was negotiated down to $960). Keep in mind that the average city dweller only makes $520 a year.

The CCP is working on putting an end to these unauthorized fees. As of the middle of September 1997, 21 provinces and cities had canceled 2,877 fees for a savings to SOEs of $1.8 billion just in 1997 (China's tax collectors on a roll at McDonald's. International Harold Tribune, September 11, 1997:17).

Since the economic boom in China, there have been a growing number of serious issues involving the abuse of power for political and personal gain and corruption by local authorities throughout the country. This is a trend that will continue as long as China clings to a legal system that can be influenced by *guanxi* instead of a rule of law that is equally applied to everyone.

The Framework of the Legal System

Focus also needs to be on the institutional framework in which the legal system operates, including the Party's view of the purpose of a legal system. This is important for a Cultural Translator to understand because the legal system that enforces the laws is even more important than the laws themselves.

Mao believed that a legal system was a tool in the hands of the ruling class—in China's case, feudal and bourgeois powers—used to oppress and exploit the workers and peasants, and to inhibit the forces of progress. The communists and traditional Chinese both saw the legal system as subordinate to a dominant political philosophy (Dreyer 1996).

The CCP believed that the system it inherited was designed to protect the rich, therefore, they destroyed the entire legal system established by the Nationalist government and created their own. The legal system that the Communists developed and used between 1949 and 1953 actually used two legal schools of thought called: jural and societal. The jural model focuses on the formal, elaborate, and codified rules enforced by a regular judicial hierarchy, while the societal model emphasizes socially approved norms and values.

Under the Common Program passed by the CPPCC in 1949, a formal legal system was established. This system was modeled after the Soviet model and established a state organ called the Procuracy. The Procuracy was founded to investigate and supervise the judicial system as well as oversee the actions of the public security (police) force that initiates the arrests and prosecution of individuals.

It also ensures that investigations follow the correct legal procedures. If the procedures are followed correctly then the procurators collect the information on those to be tried and act as the prosecutors in criminal trials (Dreyer 1996).

To assist the Procuracy in these investigations, they also keep a file, called a "dossier", on every single person in China. There are actually two identical copies of each person's dossier, the public security bureau keeps one and the person's work-unit keeps the other one. The dossier contains any and all information that could be important, including the person's pictures, family and relatives' names, school grades and transcripts, criminal record, and much more. It is the single most important document in a person's life and the individual has no access to it at any time. Therefore, an individual would never know if the information contained within the dossier was accurate or not, until it was too late. (Dreyer 1996).

The State established the structure of the legal system by creating the Public Security Bureau, the Procuracy, and a three-tiered judicial system of basic, intermediate and Supreme Court levels. In the three-tiered judicial system there is only one right of appeal. From 1949 to 1953, however, the public security bureau dispensed justice without reference to the Procuracy, the court system, or the law. They made arbitrary arrests and detentions of individuals and forced confessions from them. These individuals were then given ad hoc punishments with no appeals (Dreyer 1996).

While Mao was mobilizing the masses during campaigns such as land reform, and the anticounterrevolutionay movement, the Public Security Bureau was hastily convening people's tribunals to hand out revolutionary justice at mass trials. "Mao Zedong stated that eight hundred thousand people deemed to be reactionaries and bad elements received death sentences at such trials; other estimates run in the millions" (Dreyer 1996: 165). Others were sent to labor and re-education camps for "reform through labor." These sentences were long and the conditions at these camps were very poor. Only the very strong survived, thus making many of these death sentences as well (Christiansen 1996; Dreyer 1996).

Then, in 1954, China's first state constitution was established. This indicated that the CCP was making a commitment to the institutionalization of its rule of law. The constitution established the National People's Congress (NPC) as the highest organ of state authority. The NPC, along with its standing committee, was vested with broad powers of legislation, amendment, and appointment. The constitution also established the State Council as China's chief administrative organ. It designated the State Council, the Supreme People's Court, and the Supreme People's Procuracy as comprising the central government structure. All three were made accountable to the NPC and its standing committee, which had the power to appoint or remove its officials (Dreyer 1996).

Other articles of the constitution guaranteed equality before the law, freedom of speech, of the press, of association, of demonstration, and of religion. In addition, there were guarantees to the right to work, to leisure, to education, and to social assistance. Explicit protection against arbitrary arrest was provided by an article declaring that "freedom of the person of citizens of the PRC is inviolable. No citizen may be arrested except by decision of the people's court or the people's Procuracy" (Dreyer 1996: 166). An Arrest and Detention Act, promulgated in the same year, added concrete and detailed procedures to the guarantee. A large number of substantive and procedural laws and regulations were drawn up (Dreyer 1996).

Though the legal system was improved, it still was in a communist state with communist ideology. In keeping with the communist ideology that saw law as a tool of the ruling class, those who had been designated reactionaries or class enemies had no constitutional rights whatsoever. In other words, the constitutional guarantees of equality before the law did not mean that the law would be equally applied to all.

Then, in 1957 during the Hundred Flowers movement, the people criticized the legal system. This caused the CCP to abandon the jural model that was patterned after the Soviets. What emerged was a highly arbitrary societal model. The reasoning behind this change was the belief that the CCP's policies were the law (Dreyer 1996).

During the Cultural Revolution, Mao completely abandoned the entire legal system and had his Red Guards crush it, including the public security, the Procuracy, and the court system. The damage to society and to the legal system made it clear that the CCP needed a new constitution, and one was adopted in April 1969. The new constitution, however, did not bring an end to the Cultural Revolution or to the intraleadership fighting. Then, shortly after the

1969 constitution was adopted, the CCP believed that a new constitution needed to be adopted and suspended the one just adopted. The new constitution was not adopted until six years later in 1975 (Dreyer 1996).

Mao's death ended the Cultural Revolution, and made Deng Xiaoping the Party Leader. Under Deng, the legal system abruptly changed its emphasis once again, this time moving back toward a jural model. From an economic point of view, Deng believed that Chinese entrepreneurs needed protection for both their individual rights and those of their businesses if they were to risk breaking so sharply from past strict communist practices. Remember that a year prior people were being thrown into prison for having any type of capitalistic ideas. Now the CCP and the State were telling people that being a capitalist was a good thing. Deng even told the people that getting rich was glorious. Additionally, Deng understood that foreign companies needed the security of law and recourse for the courts to safeguard their investments.

Again in March 1978, the state adopted still another constitution, replacing the one adopted in 1975. Later in 1978, a CCP plenary meeting reaffirmed the independence of the judiciary and the equality of all people before the law, regardless of class background (Dreyer 1996). As Deng brought the CCP and the country back to stability, the new legal system was improving.

As this new legal system was put to the test and the CCP was busy making corrections to the constitution and the laws, the Party decided that it was better to adopt a new constitution than to try and ratify the old one. So, in 1982 the state adopted yet another new constitution, the one that, as far as I can tell, is still in use today. It describes China as a "People's Democratic Dictatorship." This constitution stated that the courts cannot be subject to interference by administrative organs, public organizations, or individuals. An interesting point here is that the CCP is not one of these; therefore, it is not restricted by the provision (Christiansen 1996).

It is important to point out that, in the past, when the constitution or the law got in the way of the CCP's ideology; the legal system was simply discarded. There were mass arrests during these times, and people were routinely sent to prison without trial. These times were terrible. Many ordinary citizens and high CCP officials were victim to the whims of the changing political winds that swept the CCP. That even included Deng Xiaoping, who was twice sent down by Mao. This is why Deng was in favor a stable legal system. The arbitrary disregard for a stable law and legal system is also what worries investors.

It is interesting to point out here that the People's Court of the PRC is only on the organizational flowchart of the NPC and not the CCP.

Summary

Since the founding of the PRC in 1949, its political system has gone through major transformations on several occasions, including The Hundred Flowers Bloom Campaign, the Great Leap Forward, The Cultural Revolution, and the June 4 incident. A small group, expressing power through *guanxi,* generated political power struggles over public policies and ideology, and allowed the abuse of power to go unquestioned. The resulting disorder cost the lives of tens of millions of ordinary citizens, and of some of the top CCP and State officials. This chapter examined some of the causes and effects of these power struggles by exploring these political events and the relationship of the CCP to the State and to the legal system.

As isolated events, these political conflicts are not easily understood, but once the political events, the relationship between the CCP, the State, and the legal system are considered, the true sources of the Chinese businessperson's problems start to emerge.

Deng Xiaoping realized this and knew that the PRC could never grow politically or succeed economically if things did not change; therefore, he started to distribute the power over a larger number of people within the CCP. He also established a new constitution with a jural legal system to ensure that his new policies, especially the economic ones, would succeed. These two events are the cornerstone of the PRC's current economic success, a success that can be seen in the millions of dollars that are flowing into China through foreign direct investment. Jiang Zemin has continued with these policies and has taken them even further by insisting that the PLA sell off its 20,000 plus companies and that the State sell off almost all their SOEs, either on the stock market or outright to private investors.

Since Deng came to power, the political bloodbaths seem to have eased with the redistribution of power over a wider base. The removal of CCP officials during the last reorganization appeared to happen without too many incidents. The legal system also appears to be doing better with the creation of the TIPS program and the prosecution of at least a few high-ranking local officials for corruption.

The CCP and the NPC approved all the legal systems of the past (which were later discarded when their laws conflicted with CCP policy). This left a lack of trust in a legal system, the CCP and the State in the minds of the people. A just legal system is more than just laws on the books; it is the impartial implementation of these laws and their enforcement within the framework outlined by governmental and political bodies. The current legal system does not do this because the people who operate the legal system still don't trust the CCP. This is why the current system is a mix of laws, selective enforcement, and the use of *guanxi*.

The most important aspect of the Chinese political arena to keep in mind at all times is that Chinese society operates on a system based around the four cultural complexes of *mianzi, keqi, guanxi,* and *renqing*, a system that is alive and well within the Chinese political and legal systems. This affects foreign business because, when conducting business in China, the only defense a company will have against latent intent, corruption, hidden fees, and Party involvement in the business transactions is the guidance that can be provided by a knowledgeable Cultural Translator.

Chapter 4

The Strategic Reorganization

Understanding Your Counterpart's
Economic Structure is Key to Profitability

Since 1978, China has undergone a complete strategic reorganization of its economic policies. The economic results have been very successful, making China one of the largest economies in the world. The purpose of this chapter is to provide the Cultural Translator with accurate information concerning the reorganization process by discussing the implementation of their new dual-track economic system and the resulting economic structure.

To discuss the reorganization, this chapter is divided into two parts. The first part will discuss the implementation strategy of the strategic reorganization, and the second part will discuss their new economic structure. Section one, the implementation strategy, discusses the components of decentralization, the stages of the reorganization, and the production and pricing strategy. It will also discuss regional development and how the initial economic conditions were instrumental in making the economic reorganization a success. Section two, the new economic structure, will discuss the new ownership structure and privatization.

Section One:
Implementing the Strategic Reorganization

From the end of the Communist Revolution in 1949 to Mao's death in 1976, the Chinese have attempted one major economic reform, the Great Leap Forward (1958–1960) and one major social reform, the Cultural Revolution (1966–1976). Both of these attempts were structured with command economies and both ended with catastrophic results. Then in 1976, with Mao's death and the end of the Cultural Revolution, the CCP was able to accurately assess their economic situation. They found it in ruins. The factories were outdated and inefficient, and their management techniques were based on Marxist philosophies taught during the Cultural Revolution.

They also discovered that the Bank of China (China's central bank) had been making non-performing loans to these factories over the years; but were never being paid back. This was creating a serious situation for the CCP because if the factories could not pay back the loans, then there would be runaway inflation (Woo 1997). The CA under-stood the seriousness of this economic situation and proposed a third attempt at economic reforms, called the Open Door policy in 1978. These policies were different than the ones pursued during the Great Leap and the Cultural Revolution because they were not focused on a centrally-based, command economy. Instead, they decided to revise their interpretation of Marxist ideology and develop an economy that was a combination of market and command based.

To do this, the Third Plenary Session of the Eleventh Central Committee adopted a resolution that criticized the over centralization of the State in managing its enterprises. They believed that the characteristics of a socialist economy consist, not so much of "centralizing all labor and resources in the hands of the State, but by coordinating all economic activities according to scientific forecasts" (Mathur 1987: 83). These scientific forecasts can be used to set goals for the five-year plans and for long-range programs, such as economic development.

This change in policy was really a change in the role of government from a central authority to a central source of reliable information. This would allow the CA to fix the ratios between accumulation and consumption for the State Owned Enterprises (SOEs), as well as for allocating funds for capital construction and key projects to improve the people's standard of living. The central authority (CA) believed that this type of planning was necessary because the economy would be a mixture of SOEs and private enterprises. Therefore, the two sectors would need the same reliable information to coordinate their activities accordingly (Mathur 1987).

The changes in economic policy did improve the economic situation in China considerably, as illustrated in tables 4.1–4.4. In the first year of implementation in 1979, foreign trade with China went from $20.6 billion to $135.7 billion by 1991 (Woo 1997). In 1994, the combined foreign direct investment totals from 1979 to 1994 were $63.5 billion (see Table 4.1). About 50 percent of the SOEs, however, were still operating at a loss at this time (Woo 1997). In 1997, Jiang Zemin had no choice but to approve further layoffs at the SOEs. He justified these layoffs by explaining that Marxism cannot remain unchanged and those who indulge in book worship can only lead to backwardness and even failure. China must diversify its ownership through, "reorganization, association, merger, leasing, contract operations, and joint stock partnerships or sell-off" (Mufson, Steven. Chinese get the word on reform: Jiang stressed party control as economy goes private, September 13–14, 1997:1). He later said that, "All workers should change their ideas about employment and improve their own quality to meet the new requirements of reform and development" (China's Party Leaders nod and wink at Marx; International Herald Tribune. September 19, 1997:4).

Three Control Mechanisms for the Economy

The CA did not have a set plan for implementing the reorganization of the Chinese economy[4]. They did, however, establish three control mechan-isms of administration, currency, and subsidies to ensure that they did not lose control of the economy or the reorganization.

The CA placed administrative controls on the economy to ensure that foreign trade stayed within the margins established by the annual State plan, which set the import and export targets based on need, and on the balance of payments. The admini-

---

[4] It is also important to note that a good portion of the information contained in this chapter came from a book entitled, *Economies in Transition: Comparing Asia and Europe*. This book was edited by Wing Thye Woo, a Professor of Economics at the University of California at Davis, Stephen Parker, Chief Economist at the Asia Foundation, and Jeffrey D. Sachs, Director of the Harvard Institute for International Development. The book is a collection of various papers that are well researched regarding the economic development of Asia and Eastern Europe.

strative controls were beginning to be relaxed in the early 1990s because international firms were choosing not to invest large amounts of money if they did not have some type of control over their investment. In addition, decentralizing the system has caused many of the administrative controls to weaken. Those controls did serve as a method of allowing the CA to regulate the market balance between the State and open markets.

The second control mechanism the CA implemented was the non-convertibility of their currency. China's currency lacks convertibility on the open market to a hard currency, such as the United States dollar. This non-convertibility acted as another administrative control over foreign trade. This was a major factor because, by controlling the currency, the CA was able to control inflation, devaluation, and convertibility. Due to this control of the currency, Zhu Rongji, Vice Premier, was able to state confidently that the Renminbi (Yuan) would not be devaluated, thus establishing the confidence of outside investors in the currency and the government (No currency woes here: but China must tackle SOE and banking reforms. AsiaWeek, December 19, 1997: 1).

Subsidies proved to be the final control the CA had in regulating the economy and the reorganization process. This also proved to be the most needed, as well as the most costly. By allowing the SOEs and TVEs subsidies, the CA allowed them to compete in the new open market for a fixed period to become profitable, but this added billions of Yuan to China's staggering debt load (Woo 1997).

By implementing these three control mechanisms the CA was able to control the economy by regulating the decentralization of authority, controlling the speed of the reorganization, and by controlling the production and pricing systems.

Components of Decentralization

According to Woo (1997), the decentralization of the economy in China was successful because of three components: a Budgetary Contracting System, a Contract Responsibility System, and direct borrowing.

Under the budgetary contracting system, the fiscal relationship between the CA and the local authorities was changed by the CA sharing revenues with the local authorities. This occurred in one of two ways. The first was that the CA and the local authorities collected revenues (taxes and profit remittances) according to the administrative subordinate relationship (different levels of government will tax different payers). The second method consisted of a contract between the local and central authorities regarding the amount of money each local authority would pay the central authority for a specified amount of time. If the local authority was going to fall short on their contractually agreed upon amount, then they would receive a subsidy from the CA. If they did receive subsidies from the central authority, however, the local authority would lose a certain amount of control.

The second component was a Contract Responsibility System that was introduced in 1985 for SOEs. This was a contract between the CA and the

SOE, which stated that the SOE was to pay a given amount in taxes and profits to the CA and anything above the agreed upon amount they retained for themselves.

Direct borrowing was the third component, which was also introduced in 1985. This allowed the SOEs to borrow directly from banks, employees, and other financial institutions for operating expenses and fixed asset investment. The CA allowed this type of direct borrowing because it was no longer going to supply state grants to local governments for these types of expenses.

These control mechanisms and components of decentralization were used by the CA to regulate the economy to ensure that the reforms happened gradually.

The Stages of Reorganization

This transition to a "market-oriented, outward-looking, and private-sector-led economic system" was a major undertaking for the CA. Their biggest challenge was to know what to do and when, because they never approved a "comprehensive reform blueprint with a specific timetable for implementation" (Lardy 1992:3). They instead were able to loosen or tighten economic policies when they deemed it prudent. This is probably why their transition has been so successful. They were not tied to a strict plan. They preferred the gradual method over one based on rapid and strong adjustments, known as shock therapy. The result has been smooth economic growth that occurred in four orderly stages:

1. From 1978 to 1984, economic reform was centered on the countryside;

2. From 1984 to 1988, reform was extended to the cities at a medium pace;

3. From 1988 to 1992, a macroeconomic stabilization program was implemented and the pace of reforms were slowed (Due to high inflation);

4. From 1992 to present, a medium pace of reforms resumed.

These stages were not planned; they just developed based on the needs of the CA and the market. When a situation occurred that required quick reforms to be implemented right away, the CCP responded. If the economy was running smoothly, they waited for the right time to implement more changes. The third phase was a period of slowing of the economy due to inflation. Inflation was a serious issue because the majority of the students, teachers, elderly, and unemployed were still on very small fixed incomes from the State. As the government allowed the state prices to rise to meet the market prices, they did not increase these people's monthly income, therefore inflation occurred. The situation reached critical in 1989, when students in Beijing began protesting at Tiananmen Square. This protest ended when the CA and Deng ordered the military to clear the students from Tiananmen Square on June 4, 1989 (see Chapter 3). When the production and pricing stabilized again in 1992, the reforms continued (Woo 1997).

Production and Pricing

An important factor in the transition to a dual-track economy was the production and pricing plan. The plan was simple: open the free market while keeping state supply unchanged at a lower price plan, then gradually, adjust the price and supply plans incrementally to approach the market price. This allowed the SOEs and TVEs to compete with the private sector in the marketplace by offering less expensive alternatives. It also allowed them time to modernize their facilities so they could compete directly in the marketplace.

The production and pricing plan was first implemented in 1978 with the comprehensive and rapid liberalization of the agricultural sector, however, the industrial sector remained under traditional central planning management. This turned out to be a successful formula. In 1978, the proportion of planned production of the total value of industrial output was 90 percent; by 1993 it had dropped to 5 percent. In addition, by the end of 1993 there were only 45 kinds of goods still subjected to the state-set plan prices. Among these 45 goods were the state's purchase prices of grain, cotton, and tobacco, and the state's sales prices of chemical materials, coal, electricity, oil, natural gas, chemical fertilizers, steel ingots, and cars (Woo 1997).

This plan allowed the state sectors to retain their skilled workers by offering them better benefits than the private sector could offer at the time. This kept the already employed skilled workers at their current jobs and forced the private enterprises to hire the unemployed agricultural workers from the rural areas. The results of this type of economic transformation have been good, according to the statistics.

The Chinese government is reporting that between 1978 and 1993, the agricultural work force dropped from 71 percent to 56 percent of the total workforce, and the proportion of the Gross National Product (GNP) from SOEs dropped from 78 percent to 43 percent. This economic activity also increased international trade from 10 percent to 36 percent and foreign direct investment jumped to $28 billion from $2 billion (Woo 1997).

Regional Development

In 1980, the Chinese developed four "Special Economic Zones" (SEZs) in the cities of Shantou, Shenzhen, Xiamen, and Zhuhai. These SEZs were designated as economic test areas for the "One China, Two System" approach to political and economic changes. Due to the success of these zones, in 1988, Hainan province became the fifth and final SEZ. The SEZs experienced phenomenal economic growth rates, which spurred other regions to demand economic liberalization as well. A short time later, 20 additional cities were subsequently approved as "economic and technological development districts" (ETDDs), which gave them some of the same privileges as the SEZs (Woo 1997).

These economic successes, which were located in the coastal areas, were known by the rest of the country. People also noticed that the growth did not come from state industrial reform, but from the rapid development of the non-state sector. Similar economic zones, soon dotted the entire country and more of them keep appearing. In 1991, there were 191 of these economic zones, which grew to nearly 3,000 by 1994; however, only the five SEZs "wield central-level political clout and the autonomy to approve large deals quickly and independently from outside government interference" (Engholm 1994:221).

The SEZs have been specially designed to attract foreign direct investment by allowing them to have special privileges that appeal to foreign firms. Some of these special privileges include the ability to employ foreign staff managers who, in turn, don't pay taxes and are exempt from import/export duties as well as from after-tax profit remittance. The SEZs also have access to Chinese partners, which is facilitated by various industry-specific development companies created organized to assist foreign investors. The tax rates are attractive at 15 percent in the SEZs compared to the 18.5 percent in Hong Kong (Engholm 1994).

Understanding the importance of the SEZs to the Chinese economy, Premier Li Ping met with Zhu Rongji, China's economic czar, to formulate a strategy to make the SEZs more effective. Their meeting also included the heads of three other special economic zones—Shantou, Xiamen and Hainan—where Mr. Jiang's promise that the policy on the SEZs would not change was reaffirmed. They also agreed that, to make them more effective, they had to address corruption, abuse of power, and account rigging by local officials (Chinese leaders discuss ways to make SEZs more effective. International Harold Tribune, April 4, 1996).

Special Economic Zones

As the CA was working on a new constitution and a new legal system, they were also working on a way to decentralize the foreign trade bureaucracy to protect the foreign investors and to facilitate borrowing from abroad. Though the CA wanted the new technology and cash from foreign investment, they did not want to infuse foreign cultural values into Chinese culture. To limit the foreign cultural diffusion, the CA established a new cultural "Great Wall—the Special Economic Zones or SEZs.

The idea behind the SEZs was to create a specific place where foreigners and foreign companies could conduct business in China in the fashion to which the foreign companies were accustomed. This included permitting Western televised news reports, telecommunications, transportation, and other infrastructure necessities, including the power to hire and fire Chinese personnel. The CA understood that these were necessary to attract foreign direct investment, western management experience, and new business; however, they did not believe that these things were good for all of China. They saw these foreign influences as a threat that could erode the core of Chinese culture; therefore they sought to limit and isolate the foreigners' influence from the Chinese people. The CA believed that by establishing a limited number of specific areas where the foreign companies could operate as they were accustomed, this would limit the influence of their ideas on the Chinese people.

As China enters the year 2000, the CA can look at the SEZs as a political, economic and social success. Within fifteen years of opening its economic doors, China went from a closed country to one with 116 ports for water transportation, 55 for land crossing, and 48 airports. In 1994, China handled 330 million tons of foreign goods; that is up almost 8 percent from the previous year. The number of airline passengers reached 101.22 million, up almost 6 percent. Additionally, foreign companies have signed about 324,620 foreign direct investment contracts worth about \$267,315 million (see Table 4.1).

One of the goals of the SEZ-format was to create a place where foreign companies could build their manufacturing facilities for the purpose of adding value to their product and then export the products out of China. This is one reason why the CA was focusing on high-tech industries. Table 4.4 illustrates that 56 percent of the utilized contractual agreements are in the manufacturing industry. Though this is impressive, China still has not been able to attract the high-tech items it wants, instead, they have attracted the low-tech, high manual labor jobs.

Though the SEZs have been a success for certain areas and industries of China, they have also demonstrated their limitations according to Joseph Battat, an officer of the World Bank Development. "China has not been able to attract the high-technology projects it wants, the actual foreign investment utilized is only half of that contracted, and, except in a few coastal provinces, the impact of foreign direct investment on the domestic economy has been inconsequential" (De Keijzer 1992: 37). While Joseph Battat is correct in his assessment, it must not take away from what the CA has been able to accomplish in just fifteen years.

Sources of Growth

Woo (1997) argues that there are five important factors involved in the successful economic expansion of China between 1978 and 1994. Two of the factors, integration into the global economy, and a high rate of individual savings, are considered general lessons in economic reform. While the other three factors, the structural features and initial conditions, the Chinese Diaspora, and the Great Leap and the Cultural Revolution are considered as circumstances unique to China.

Integration into the Global Economy

The integration into the global economy assisted China in three ways. First, it provided access to international markets, which allowed China to attract labor-intensive, low-tech, manufacturing jobs. This, in turn, accelerated the movement of labor out of the low-productivity agriculture jobs and into high-productivity industry jobs (Woo 1997). Second, it gave China the access to purchase modern technology. The third factor was the access to foreign direct investment, which gave local companies access to global distribution networks and more efficient management techniques, as well as to capital stock (equipment) and new technology.

High Rate of Individual Savings

A second factor in China's economic success was its high rate of individual savings. In China, the individual saving rates are about 23 percent of disposable income, which is extremely high, compared to the 21 percent in Japan, 18 percent in Taiwan, and only 8 percent in the United States. The money in these saving accounts was actually being injected back into the economy through the banking system at an increasing rate over time. In 1980, the loans were equal to about 3.2 percent of the GDP, however by 1991, the figure rose to 11.7 percent (Woo 1997).

The high household saving reduced the rate of inflation in the Chinese economy through two channels. The first channel was that the savings were in the form of currency, which causes a higher demand for the currency. What this means is that the majority of Chinese placed their disposable money (money they can afford to spend after all the bills are paid) into their savings accounts. In other words, they did not spend it therefore it did not get recycled into the economy. By the majority of Chinese doing this, the actual currency began to be in short supply. On my first trip to China, in Guangzhou there was actually a shortage of one RMB denominations. If something cost less than 5 RMB, you could not get change. This being the case, people, including myself, collected small denominations of RMB, which placed the currency in high demand. This high demand for the currency was one factor in keeping the inflation low.

The second factor was due to the savings being in currency. This reduced the need for the government to print money to meet the excessive resource demand of the SOE sector. What this means is that in order for the Bank of China to loan currency to the SOEs, the government would either need to print additional money, which would cause inflation. Or they would need to find somewhere else to borrow the money to loan to the SOEs. Therefore, the CA borrowed the money from the people's savings accounts in the Bank of China and lent it to the SOEs, which used the money to pay their bills, including payroll. Their employees then paid their bills and put the rest into their savings accounts, which the CA then borrowed again to lend the SOEs. This cycle gave the CA a large resource of currency, which prevented the CA from printing more money.

Initial Economic Conditions

The initial economic conditions in China are arguably the most important factors behind the economic growth because they allowed the economy to develop gradually. Woo (1997) has argued that the initial economic conditions of a country are deciding factors if an economy is going to develop gradually. Woo stated that, "Gradualism is more likely to succeed in an underdeveloped (under-industrialized) economy with a huge surplus rural labor force, like China, than in an "over-industrialized" economy dominated by the state sector, like Poland or Russia" (Woo 1997:28).

One of the initial economic conditions in China that allowed it to develop gradually was that the agricultural sector comprised 71 percent of the labor force in 1978. This condition provided an enormous supply of labor for the new economy because the peasants did not receive the types of benefits that the SOE workers received, and they only consumed about one-third the amount that urban residents consumed. Peasants, therefore, were eager to trade-in their low-paying agricultural job for a higher paying job in the TVEs.

The primary cause of the economic growth in China was due to the low-productivity agricultural labor moving to higher-productivity jobs in TVEs. This, however, was only one of three initial economic conditions that assisted in the economic growth in China in the 1980s. Another condition was the size of the centralized planning effort. In China, the planned economy was about 1,200 commodities compared to Russia with about 25 million commodities. The third condition was the lack of large external debt. The lack of external economic pressure meant that China could develop its economy at its own pace, gradually (Woo 1997).

Debilitating Mass Campaigns

Woo (1997) has suggested that the intraleadership fighting during the Great Leap (1958–1962) and the Cultural Revolution (1966–1976) assisted the economic growth in China by discrediting centralized planning. The Cultural Revolution also displaced about 75 percent of the CCP members who were in positions of power. This created a void of political opposition allowing Deng to make his political appointments quickly and without much intraleadership fighting. Through these appointments, Deng was able to make the political changes needed to rebuild the Chinese political and economic systems.

The Chinese Diaspora

The existence of family ties between the mainland Chinese and the overseas Chinese has been instrumental in the new economic success of China. The explosive growth of the SEZs was due to overseas Chinese moving their labor-intensive industries from Hong Kong and Taiwan to southern China (Woo 1997). In addition, they utilized family connections that "greatly reduced the transaction costs of the investment by providing reliable local supervisors, inside information on the enforcement of regulations, and contact with the local authorities" (Woo 1997: 31).

Section Two: The New Economic Structure

The purpose of this section is to provide a brief but clear explanation of the new ownership structures of the TVEs and the SOEs, and of the role of privatization in the new economic structure. Clarification is necessary because the new ownership structure is not clear, but it is one of the most important reform components of the dual-track economic system. The lack of clarity of the new economic system can be seen in how the public sector is defined by Xian Bensi, Vice President of the Party School of the Central Committee of Communist Party of China. "The public sector includes not only the

State sector but also the collective sector, and the collective sector is also the public sector, and the State- and collectively-owned elements is the sector of mixed ownership and also belongs to the public sector" (Ownership form and democracy should accord with national conditions, say theorists. Electronic document, http://www.chinadaily.net/cndy/ history/ 15/own.html, accessed, November 27 1997). Clearly the new economic structure is not clear.

Under the new system, individuals are allowed to own property, such as homes, private business, and buildings, as well as bridges, hospitals, and stock in companies—something never heard of under the old communist system. Deng and the CA understood that the old public-ownership structure would need to change if China was going to update and modernize almost a hundred-thousand SOEs and over 7 million TVE facilities.

Town and Village Enterprises

The TVEs were originally factories that were developed in the rural communes during the Great Leap and the decade-long Cultural Revolution. The majority of these factories were built because the Cultural Revolution caused a nationwide collapse of the distribution system; therefore, the communes had to expand their non-agricultural activities into manufacturing products that they could no longer have delivered. The result was the development of over 7 million factories spread out over rural China. Now these factories are called TVEs and are equivalent to local factories that manufacture a range of products. Any specific information regarding TVEs is difficult to obtain because the ownership and control structures are difficult to define, they span a wide variety of industries, and have an evolving nature (Woo 1997).

Today these TVEs are classified as non-state enterprises even though they are, for the most part, controlled by the local governments. They are classified as non-state because of the ownership structure, not the control structure. Under the private enterprise system, there are three main types of ownership structures for the TVEs. The first form is the Jiangsu Model, where local authorities exercise tight control of the movement of labor and pay. The Zhejiang Model is the second form of TVE. In this model, the TVE makes annual contributions to the village funds and the local authorities are the majority, but silent stockholders in most of these TVEs. The third major type of ownership is generally known as a "Red Cap". A Red Cap is a privately-owned enterprise that is owned by an individual or a small group of investors, but operates like Zhejiang-model TVEs though they are not collectively owned or operated. These enterprises act like Chinese-owned and operated companies, yet they are privately owned. The Red Cap agrees to pay a high fee or tax to the local authorities to be classified as a regular TVE. They agree to this arrangement for the special benefits, which include staying in the good graces of the CCP and being able to conduct business with fewer restrictions. The pressure on an enterprise to become a Red Cap was so great that in the province of Hebei there were 1000 private business, but only 8 registered, the rest were Red Caps (Woo 1997).

Overall, the entire TVE system is very vital to the state's economy. There are over 7 million TVEs, which employ tens of millions of people. In 1998, they accounted for more than 2.2 trillion Yuan (US$265 billion) in goods and services, which is about one-third of the Gross Domestic Product (Cui Ning 1999, Woo 1997).

State Owned Enterprise

Privatization was allowed by the CA to introduce elements of a market economy within the existing system of centralized property rights. This was accomplished by first dividing the TVEs from the SOEs in the structure of property rights. The local authorities were, in essence, given the TVEs, while the State retained the ownership of the SOEs, but allowed them autonomy.

Under this arrangement, the SOEs were given the right to retain a portion of their profits and dispense them for bonus and welfare expenditures. During the first part of this transition, managers spent all the profits by handing out large bonuses and social benefits to the employees. The managers' rationale was that, if the SOE fell short on its expectations, the State would be there with a check to bail them out. Later the CA placed limits on the bonuses and social benefits that the SOEs could provide employees.

In addition to being able to keep a portion of their profits, the SOEs were able to sell a portion of their output in the free market, to introduce new products, and to raise funds for investments of its own choice. They also had two additional rights that they have almost never used: the right to fire workers and the right to file bankruptcy. These two rights should be exercised more often because in 1994, about 50 percent of the SOEs ran operational losses (Woo 1997).

Another reason for these changes in the ownership policy was that the CA was planning to sell-off the smaller non-performing SOEs. To accomplish this, the CA needed to be able to transfer ownership and management responsibilities away from the state and onto private investors. Under the old public ownership structure, this was not possible. The CA was planning to reduce the number of SOEs from about 100,000 to around 500 large, strategic ones. These 500 large SOEs would account for about half of the State sector's total assets and sales (Mufson 1997).

This change of attitude toward the smaller enterprises was being called a "survival of the fittest" attitude. One of the reasons why the State has taken this "survival of the fittest" attitude has to do with the state's ability to make profits. Currently less than 1 percent of the SOEs are successful giant firms. 70 percent of state owned firms are running at a loss and 35 percent have debts greater than assets. A change to a market economy cannot occur quickly because there are approximately 100 million urban workers in this sector, and a sudden loss of state support would displace millions of workers. Such a rapid transformation could cause great unrest (China reform is long-term and gradual, officials say. International Herald Tribune, September 15, 1997:2).

Therefore, the diversification of ownership of SOEs, according to Prime Minister Li Peng, needs to be implemented slowly and cautiously. He was quoted in the International Herald Tribune on September 15, 1997 as saying to the Xinhua news agency, "Work in this regard should be done according to the law of the market economy and be gradually standardized". This is because "the planned ownership reorganization aims to create incentives for improved management and performance, but analysts say it cannot produce a turnaround overnight, especially for firms buried under mountains of debt" (China reform is long-term and gradual, officials say. International Herald Tribune, September 15, 1997:2).

The Difference between SOEs and TVEs

The biggest difference between a SOEs and TVEs is that TVEs "represent localized socialism compared to the centralized socialism embodied by the SOEs" (Woo 1997:25). This distinction might appear minor because legally, they are both publicly owned and subject to regulation, but it does have a major effect on how they operate. In this respect, the SOEs and TVEs have three major differences: the distance from supervision, state vs. non-state enterprises, and the potential for innovation.

The distance from supervision is critical when dealing with TVEs because, for the most part, they only have to answer to local authorities. While SOEs are, for the most part, autonomous, they do answer to the CA.

There are additional advantages in dealing with TVEs as well. There is a direct link between them and the local people, which has some economic advantages, such as reducing the cost of supervision. The local owners have an economic incentive to monitor the management, and they have the ability to exert pressure on the managers to improve the business. Workers also have the ability to complain about excessive managerial appropriations of resources (Woo 1997).

Under this reorganization, the TVEs now fall under the control and authority of the local authority, not the CA. Since the TVEs no longer fall under the CA, they are classified a non-state enterprise and, as such, they are no longer protected from bankruptcy and no longer have access to the endless supply of state money to cover their losses. It is now the local governments' or investors' responsibility to ensure profitability.

With the new authority structure and non-state status, TVEs are able to implement institutional innovations faster than SOEs because they don't require the CA's approval. Thus, decisions can be made and implemented quickly. This ability to innovate will be critical if the TVEs are going to compete in a more open economic market without the support of the State. One of the advantages they have is the ability to update their facilities faster than the larger SOEs, an ability they will need since they are driven by market forces. They are driven more by market forces than the SOE because there are over 7 million of them, but in total they represent a smaller portion of the overall economy than the SOEs. This is due to their place in the CA's overall plan. The SOEs are to be constants in the overall planned economy; therefore they cannot be as affected by market forces as the TVEs. As a result, the number of industrial TVEs fell from 7.7 million in 1988 to 7.2 million in 1990, while the number of SOEs grew from 99,000 to 104,000 during the same time period (Woo 1997). From 1978 to 1993, the SOEs employed 18 percent of the labor force, while adding about 35 million more workers (Woo 1997).

Privatization

Privatization has been good for China, but it has been especially good for the People's Liberation Army or PLA. By the early to mid-1990s, the People's Liberation Army or PLA owned an estimated 20,000 companies with total profits reaching as high as $5 billion (Naisbitt 1997). Their holdings are diversified and it is estimated that about half of the Chinese military personal are active in some commercial enterprise. This has made the PLA the largest privatization project in the world (Naisbitt, 1997). Even well-known American companies are working with the PLA. Citicorp has invested in their 999 Pharmaceutical Company, and Baskin Robbins works through a PLA-owned company to sell its ice cream. They also own hotels, bars, bus routes, and China United Airlines.

Though privatization has been successful for the PLA, they are the exception, not the rule. They are the exception because the "rules of the game" generally don't apply to them. For example, they use their military aircraft and airports to move products and people all over China, while other companies in China are limited to the unreliable civilian modes of transportation.

In general, the overall success of privatization has been slow and questionable. The main reason has to do with the CA's purpose in allowing privatization in China. Their plan was to use privatization for two purposes, to remove debt and to gain capital. To remove the over $200 billion in debt, the CA needs to sell-off the causes of the debt, which are the TVEs and the smaller SOEs. This will remove a tremendous cash drain from the government. This also does not pose a threat to the CA concerning losing control of the economy, because the TVEs and smaller SOEs only make up about 25 to 40 percent of the GDP.

The second purpose was to raise the needed capital to modernize the larger SOEs. This was to be accomplished by offering the companies' stock on the open market. They are expecting to raise $40 billion a year in foreign investment by selling 130,000 SOEs. The CA is only planning to sell a minority interest, in the larger SOEs. This will allow them to retain the majority share and the control of the companies, and to retain control of the economy. According to Long Yongtu, the Deputy Minister of Foreign Trade and Economic Cooperation, the larger SOEs are the backbone of the economy, accounting for about 75 percent of the GDP (Gage 1997).

The CA, with its defined purpose for the privatization of the TVEs and the smaller SOEs, has focused on the development of three categories of value-added export products and manufactured goods: electronics assembly, pharmaceuticals, and machine tools (De Keijzer 1992). Investors in the West are focusing on three investment areas as well, however they are different than the Chinese priorities. The first focus is on projects that make new machinery, material, and equipment that can be marketed domestically and internationally. The second focus is on projects that upgrade existing products, increase their variety, and make them more competitive on the world market. The third investment priority for foreign investors is on projects related to building China's infrastructure, either by producing materials now in short supply or that are related to energy, communications, transportation, and agriculture (De Keijzer 1992).

The CA officials have realized that there is a conflict in their overall goals and those of the investors in the West, but they have welcomed the foreign investment for two reasons. The first is that China needs to further diversify its exports and move into value-added goods, since foreign-owned companies and foreign joint ventures accounted for a full 47 percent of China's exports (Gage 1997).

The second reason is the staggering internal debt, which grew by almost 90 billion Yuan (the Yuan is the Chinese equivalent to the US dollar) in 1996 alone. In addition, the Bank of China (China's Central Bank) has reported that the amount of past-due loans over two years rose 20 percent in the first half of 1997, to a staggering US $17.2 billion (China steers firms to private financing, International Herald Tribune, September 11, 1997). Therefore, China is willing to make concessions in their overall plan to reduce the debt.

These situations have motivated the CA to allow two major forms of foreign investment in China, joint ventures (JVs), and the stock market. In the beginning, the CA laid out three forms of joint ventures, equity, contractual, and wholly foreign owned. The stock market is the newest form of investment and is focused on assisting the larger SOEs in raising capital to modernize their facilities (DeKeijzer 1995).

Joint Ventures

Equity joint ventures are the most successful and are favored by the CA with tax incentives. An equity joint venture would lower its tax burden from 50 percent to 33 percent. The JVs' equity is through joint stock ownership and its purpose is for the production of a specific product. Each side would contribute various assets to the enterprise. The Chinese typically contributed their equity in the form of land, a factory, infrastructure, some machinery and material, as well as labor. On occasion, they contribute cash. The foreign partner is expected to provide the technology, capital, equipment and machinery, external marketing expertise, management, and possibly additional working capital. The CA placed a minimum foreign investment at 25 percent. Control of the joint venture is through a joint board and generally the Chinese control at least 51 percent. The second type of joint venture, a contractual JV, is very similar to the equity JV. The foreign investors provide their share in the form of technology, machines, etc., and they are repaid at a set rate of return.

In view of the number of companies from the Virgin and Cayman Islands, it is important to note that many companies are registered there for tax considerations (see Table 4.3). It is also important to point out that some Chinese firms, based in China, will choose to register in Hong Kong for special consideration as well.

Table 4.1

Contractual and Utilized Foreign Direct Investment in China from All sources (1979–1998)

Year	No. of New Contracts	Contractual FDI	Utilized FDI
1979–82	920	4,958	1,769
1983	638	1,917	916
1984	2,166	2,875	1,419
1985	3,073	6,333	1,956
1986	1,498	3,330	2,244
1987	2,233	3,709	2,314
1988	5,945	5,297	3,194
1989	5,779	5,600	3,393
1990	7,273	6,596	3,487
1991	12,978	11,977	4,366
1992	48,764	58,124	11,008
1993	83,437	111,436	27,515
1994	47,549	82,680	33,767
1995	37,011	91,282	37,521
1996	24,556	73,276	41,726
1997	21,001	51,003	45,257
1998	19,799	52,102	45,463
Total	**324,620**	**572,495**	**267,315**

(Millions of USD)
(Source: China 1999 Investment Climate, Part 2.)

Table 4.2

U.S. Contractual and Utilized Foreign Direct Investment in China (1979–1998)

Year	Number of New Contracts	Contractual FDI	Utilized FDI
1979–82	21	281	13
1983	25	470	5
1984	62	165	256
1985	100	1,152	357
1986	102	541	326
1987	104	342	263
1988	269	370	236
1989	276	641	284
1990	357	358	456
1991	694	548	323
1992	3,265	3,121	511
1993	6,750	6,813	2,063
1994	4,223	6,010	2,491
1995	3,474	7,471	3,083
1996	2,517	6,915	3,443
1997	2,188	4,937	3,239
1998	2,238	6,484	3,898
Total	**26,664**	**46,619**	**21,247**

(Millions of USD)
(Source: China 1999 Investment Climate, Part 2).

Table 4.3

China's Contractual and Utilized Foreign Direct Investment by Country (1998)

Country	Number of New Contracts	Contractual FDI	Utilized FDI
Hong Kong	7,805	17,613	18,508
Virgin Is.	622	6,136	4,031
U. S.	2,238	6,484	3,898
Singapore	566	3,002	3,404
Japan	1,198	2,274	3,400
Taiwan	2,970	2,982	2,915
Korea	1,309	1,641	1,803
U. K.	220	1,682	1,175
Germany	208	2,375	737
Thailand	97	563	719
France	201	489	715
Macao	264	307	422
Malaysia	144	32.6	340
Cayman Is.	41	793	324
Canada	416	947	316
Others	1,500	4,015	2,754
Total	**19,799**	**52,102**	**45,463**

(Millions USD)
(Source: China 1999 Investment Climate, Part 2).

Though these tables don't illustrate it, the overseas Chinese are responsible for a good portion of the capital invested in China through Hong Kong, Taiwan, Macao, Malaysia, Thailand, and Singapore.

Table 4.4

China's Contractual and Utilized Foreign Direct Investment by Sector (1998)

Industry	Number of New Contracts	Contractual FDI	Utilized FDI
Agriculture, Forestry, Animal Husbandry, Fisheries	876	1,204	624
Mining	168	852	578
Manufacturing	13,477	30,827	25,582
Utilities	142	1,968	3,103
Construction	318	1,750	2,064
Transport, Warehousing Postal, and Telecomm. Svcs.	274	2,301	1,645
Wholesale and Retail Trade and Food Service	1,184	1,314	1,181
Real Estate	834	6,647	6,410
Social Services	1,634	3,012	2,963
Health Care, Sports and Social Welfare	40	142	97
Education, Culture, Arts, Radio, Film, and Television Industry	14	22	68
Scientific Research and Comp. Technical Services	169	156	39
Other	669	1,906	1,108
Total	**19,799**	**52,102**	**45,463**

(Millions USD)

(Source: China 1999 Investment Climate, Part 2)

The third type of joint venture is the wholly foreign owned enterprise or WFOE. It is a limited liability entity organized solely for the benefit of the foreign company. In the beginning, many companies tried to establish WFOEs to avoid having a Chinese partner who they did not understand. This closed-minded approach made it difficult to establish such enterprises, and the ones that were established have almost all failed.

Given the political, social, and economic condition in China between 1978 and 1993, a high failure rate was to be expected in any case. Mao recently died, ending the Cultural Revolution, and Deng was trying to establish a legal system, including a new constitution. This was not the best time to go it alone in China. In 1986, just eight years after China started its "Open Door" policy, there were only 18 WFOEs, but by the end of 1990 there were over 1,800. This significant increase did not go unnoticed by the CCP or by other foreign investors looking to China (De Keijzer 1995).

This increase was so dramatic that it was a main topic at the "Strategic Relationships Conference" in China. This trend was not unique to China, but was happening all over the world. This increase in WFOEs was due to their "cost-effective means for companies to access new markets, to grow and compete," without the significant investment risk associated with the failure rates of IJVs (Strategic partnership hailed. China Daily, June 22, 1999:5). In the case of China, Henry Chow, Chairman of IBM China Co. Ltd. insisted that joint ventures do have their advantages if the two partners smoothly collaborate and share their strong points. In an article, "Strategic partnership hailed" in the *China Daily* on June 22, 1995, Henry Chow stressed the importance of the joint venture for companies entering in the Chinese market. Additionally he said, "I believe that joint ventures will continue to be established (in China) in the future, though probably out of different considerations from those of recent or in the past". He also said that, when finding a long-term strategic partner it is essential to take the time and find one that works.

The Stock Market

The second form of ownership is the stock market via H-shares. The purpose of the Chinese stock market is to allow the State to raise capital for their larger SOEs, without losing control of the economy.

As of today, this is not a recommended method for investing in China because there are only a limited number of Chinese companies listed on the exchange. In addition, they have had their problems. Tsingao Brewery went public and raised more than $100 million to build breweries, but they ended up giving a huge chunk to ailing Chinese companies in the form of non-performing loans (Jacob 1995).

There are good economic reasons for using caution when investing in China. The first is that the CA will maintain a majority ownership position in the companies, thus allowing the CA to maintain an open economy, but with Chinese characteristics. One of these Chinese characteristics will be concerned with social welfare. This will allow the CA to use the profits to keep people employed, pay for other social benefits, and to support smaller debt-ridden SOEs through acquisitions.

As far as the international community is concerned, China's external economic condition looks good. They have a minimal international debt of $45 billion as of the mid-1990s. In 1980 China was granted admission into the World Bank Group, which includes the International Monetary Fund (IMF), International Bank for Reconstruction and Development, International Development Association, and the International Finance Corporation. In 1989, they were able to obtain membership in the Asian Development Bank. In 1983, they were granted observer status in the General Agreement of Tariffs and Trade (GATT).

Challenges Facing the Reorganization

The reorganization of the Chinese economy has brought about several successes for China, however it has also brought with it some challenges including tax revenue problems, the nation's long-term security, and personal property rights issues. Their hardest challenge, however, will be the culture change from Stalinist Socialism to one that is based on a market economy, because many of their problems are the direct result of their culturally presuppositions.

Since the Communist Revolution (1949) and especially during the Great Leap Forward (1956–1958) and the Cultural Revolution (1966–1976), the Chinese cultural mindset has been programmed by the CCP along the lines of Stalin's socialism. The CCP's cultural programming stressed what the Chinese could think and how they could act, with dire consequences for any behavior that violated what the CCP considered correct. This was especially true during the period of the Cultural Revolution and the era of the Red Guards, when the definition of correct behavior was very subjective and changed to fit the given situation.

The current management situation is that almost all the managers' attitudes and values were developed during this time; therefore, they are based on Stalin's socialist ideals and the terror and uncertainty associated with that period. Then, during the Cultural Revolution, their mindsets became even more entrenched in the politicized realities associated with Mao's Thought. Mao dictated that any behavior associated with the old or capitalist ways of doing almost anything was met with long-term stays at re-education camps in the countryside and/or prison.

These managers' cultural mindsets, therefore, were crafted within the framework of a centrally planned economy with passive individuals who did not ask questions or worry about conditions they were told not to worry about by the CA. The managers were indoctrinated with a centralized plan economy theory that told the managers to worry only about meeting the output quotas. The local managers were told not to worry about the factors that make a market-based economy work, such as market, prices, resources, or input. They have also learned, as chapters two and three have pointed out, not to stick their necks out, or to believe the government. Overcoming this programming has proven to be one of the greatest challenges of the reorganization for the CA and local authorities.

The challenge they are facing is the reprogramming of these hundreds of thousands of Chinese managers not to worry about meeting output quotas, but instead to worry about the market, prices, resources, input, and quality. This is a challenge because it goes against the mindset of a lifetime. Overcoming this challenge is critical to the success of the new private enterprises.

Another challenge facing the local authorities is the actual success of the reorganization. As China moved towards a more market-based economy, there was a narrowing of the preferential treatment gap between how the State treated TVEs compared to private enterprises. The result has been a predictable one—an increase in the number of private enterprises or WFOEs choosing not to register as "Red Caps".

This situation is causing concerns for local authorities because they are now confronted with the challenge of making up the lost revenue from privatized enterprises choosing not to register as Red Caps. This loss of revenue also places some serious concerns on the long-term security of the entire community. This is of concern because the privatized TVEs are no longer under the local authority's control, and as such, they might fail, have a massive lay-off, or worst yet, not be able to meet their tax obligations. These are very real fears regarding their unknown futures.

Part of this fear is due to the Stalinist socialist ideals that have been promoted for the past fifty years—an entire lifetime, for many Chinese managers. This has made the local authorities believe that the private enterprises are wrong and harmful to the community. Therefore, the local authorities want the private enterprises to either pay a high "divorce" type settlement for the TVEs or they want the TVEs to merge with other state-run enterprises (China's Party Leaders nod and wink at Marx. International Herald Tribune, September 19, 1997:4).

A final major concern for both the CA and the local authorities is the meaning of "publicly owned". As the Chinese economy improves and people can afford to move, who will own the local factory? The community? According to the new polices from the CA, the local people own the local factory and the local authority is responsible to ensure that it is run properly. The problem stems from ownership. If the people own the factory, what happens to a person's shares when he or she moves away? Does the local authority buy the shares back, or do the people have the right to retain these shares? When people move to a new town, are they able to acquire ownership in the local factory or not? These are the types of issues that are starting to emerge and are creating ownership challenges for the CA.

Chapter 5

Business Strategies and Tactics

"Sun-Tzu said, One who excels at warfare seeks [victory] through the strategic configuration of power (shih), not from reliance of men. Thus he is able to select men and employ strategic power (shih)" (Saywer 1994: 188).

This book has stressed the importance of understanding the Chinese cultural mindset in order to successfully conduct business in China, but the Cultural Translator must also understand the Chinese business strategies and tactics to win at the negotiation table. They need to understand Chinese strategies and tactics in order to formulate counterstrategies and tactics. This chapter, therefore, will examine the strategies of Sun-Tzu and the 36 Strategies and will discuss how the Chinese use these military strategies during the negotiation process. The tactics of the Chinese negotiators will also be analyzed by examining how they use deception, time, technology, and culture to their strategic advantage. This chapter will also discuss how the foreign company can use the Central Authority's (CA) priorities and the four cultural complexes as counterstrategies and tactics during the negotiation process.

A Cultural Translator needs to understand the Asian businessperson's mindset, especially Chinese and Japanese, because the Asian businessperson believes that those who shape the economic policies of their nations should understand that what they do has the same vital importance as the conduct of war (Chu 1990). The Cultural Translator also needs to stress to the other team members that this is not an exaggeration, but reality. Due to this belief—that business should be treated as a type of corporate warfare—the Chinese businesspersons will apply military strategies to business situations, including the negotiation process. This section will address the two most famous military philosophies in China—Sun-Tzu and the 36 Strategies.

It is one of the premises of this book that by understanding a counterpart's mindset, which includes the strategies he or she is most likely to utilize during business negotiations, the Cultural Translator can have the proper contingency plan ready to turn their counterpart's strategy against them, thus obtaining the strategic advantage during the negotiation process.

This strategy was adopted from Sun-Tzu, whose strategies are famous throughout all of China and Asia. Sun-Tzu said, "Thus it is said, that one who knows the enemy and knows himself will not be endangered in a hundred engagements. One who does not know the enemy but knows himself, will sometimes be victorious, sometimes meet with defeat. One who knows neither the enemy nor himself will invariably be defeated in every engagement" (Sawyer

1994:179). I found this idea profoundly interesting in view of the 50-percent failure rate of IJVs (Zeira 1995). This single thought from the fourth century tells us why understanding a counterpart's mindset is critical in obtaining a strategic advantage during business negotiations. Part of understanding their mindset is knowing what business strategies they will utilize during the negotiation process.

Sun-Tzu's strategies and the 36 Strategies are famous because they are not about deploying troops, but about how to handle your enemy. They have been utilized by Chinese, Japanese, and Asian business-persons throughout Asia for over a thousand years. Given this regional belief—that business is war—Sun-Tzu is required reading for any business-person planning on conducting business anywhere in Asia. These strategies are an integral part of the Chinese business mindset and an understanding of them will assist the Cultural Translator in grasping how his or her counterpart thinks. The sections that follow are only an introduction to these strategies and not a comprehensive explanation of each one of them; however a few of each are discussed.

Sun-Tzu

In China, a collection of military strategies is called a *Bing Fa*. Sun-Tzu's *Bing Fa* was wrongfully translated by the West to mean *"The Art of War"*. Sun-Tzu, who lived during the fourth century, was not the only ancient Chinese military strategist. Throughout Chinese history there have been several famous military strategists, such as Han Xin, Li Chin, and Sun Pin, however, the most famous military strategist in history was Sun-Tzu. It is said that when the emperor used Sun-Tzu's strategies, they never failed. One of the reasons why his strategies have been successful has to do with how he developed his strategies. He believed that there are five elements that need to be examined when formulating a strategy.

Sun-Tzu's Five Elements of Developing a Strategy

Sun-Tzu not only teaches the strategy, but he also discusses the five elements that he considers to be needed in formulating a successful military strategy. His five elements are taken from Sawyer's (1994) translation of Sun Tzu's, *The Art of War* and from Chinning Chu's (1995) book, *The Asian Mind Game*.

THE FIVE ESSENTIAL COMPONENTS OF VICTORY

1. Know when to fight and when not to fight
2. Obtain the wholehearted support of your troops
3. Be well prepared to seize favorable opportunities
4. Free yourself from interference from superiors
5. When the time is right, act swiftly and decisively
(Chu 1991:27–40)

The first of the five elements is a moral cause. This is referring to a just cause that unites a group of people together. In the PRC's case, it is difficult to find a uniting cause because of its immense size and its historical focus on provincial concerns, rather than on national concerns. However, the CA is administering the Foreign Direct Investment (FDI) in China under a national strategy whose goal is to make China self-reliant.

The second element is temporal conditions. This refers to accepting nature's timing of events and conditions because they are uncontrollable. This is also a reason why contracts in China are viewed in the present, because conditions change and some situations are uncontrollable, therefore the agreement needs to adjust with the conditions.

The third element is the geographical conditions. In business, this refers to the inherent advantages and disadvantages that a business has in a marketplace, which it must understand and accept. The Cultural Translators not only need to understand their company's market advantages and disadvantages, but they also need to understand their counterpart's strengths and weaknesses and how to exploit these positions to achieve an economic victory.

Leadership is the fourth element. As a great military leader needs certain qualities to lead the troops, so also does a business leader. The qualities of trust, wisdom, benevolence, strictness, sincerity, and courage are needed to carry out company policies as well as to gain the respect of the workers.

The final element that Sun-Tzu believed was needed in creating a successful military strategy was organization and discipline. Sun-Tzu teaches that clear organization is needed and that the troops must have the discipline to follow the requests of their superiors exactly or chaos will result.

Sun-Tzu said, "There are no generals who have not heard of these five. Those who understand them will be victorious; those who do not understand them will not be victorious" (Sawyer 1994:167).

Sun-Tzu's Strategies

Sun-Tzu's strategies presented here come directly from Chinning Chu's (1991) book, *The Asian Mind Game.* I have chosen to use Chu's titles for Sun-Tzu's strategies because Sun-Tzu did not provide such titles for his strategies.

It is important for the Cultural Translator to understand these strategies and be able to anticipate them and to recognize them when they are used.

SUN-TZU'S STRATEGIES

1. War is a game of deception.
2. If one is able and strong, then one should disguise oneself in the order to appear inept and week.
3. When you are ready to attack, you must convey the impression that you will not attack.
4. When you are close, pretend you are far, but when you are far, you must give the illusion that you are close.
5. One should bait the enemy with small gains.
6. If the enemy is well prepared, strong, well trained, and secure in all areas, avoid a direct confrontation.
7. Create opportunities for victory by arousing your opponent's anger and causing him to take foolish actions.
8. Make your enemy grow proud and arrogant by expression of humility and weakness.
9. When your opponent is inactive, give him no rest.
10. Destroy the enemy's alliances, leaving him totally alone.
11. Victory is determined before the battle begins.

SUN-TZU'S STRATEGIES *(continued)*

12. The highest form of victory is to conquer by strategy.
13. The opportunity for victory is provided by the enemy.
14. The combination of basic elements into unique strategies.
15. Use local guides.
16. Keep plans hidden and impenetrable; move like a thunderbolt.
17. Attack when the opponent is least prepared and least expects it.
18. When the enemy speaks peace, he is plotting deception.
19. When facing death, the struggle for survival will give new birth.
20. The necessity for espionage.
    (Chu 1991:27-40)

The following are four explanations of Sun-Tzu's strategies. Their purpose is to show how to extract the fundamental meanings of his strategies and how to apply them to a modern business environment.

1. *War, a game of deception*

Sun-Tzu stresses deceiving the opponent to obtain a strategic advantage; therefore, deception plays a vital role in Chinese business strategy. This can be seen in the 25–50-percent failure rate of IJVs due to cases of hidden agendas and latent intents (Zeira 1995).
To Americans, the concept of deception does not appear heroic or ethical. This is a *cultural difference* in ethics because to Asians, including Chinese, the ability to mislead an adversary is admirable (Chu 1991).

4. When you are close, pretend you are far, but when you are far, you must give the illusion that you are close.

Sun-Tzu means to hide the point of attack from the opponent to prevent them from concentrating their forces on that point. The same is true in business negotiations. If the two parties are in negotiations and are not close to making a deal, deceive the counterpart by acting as if a deal is close to being reached. This will keep their interest in the deal and it might prove to be a good bargaining chip as well. The purpose here is to keep the counterpart at the negotiation table and make a deal. If the two sides are close to a deal, however, act as if the deal may not go through. The counterpart may give up more in the negotiation process to ensure the negotiations continue, but if they don't reach an agreement, then the Chinese company can act as if they are willing to sacrifice a great deal for the success of the contract.

5. One should bait the enemy with small gains

Sun-Tzu is counting on greed and so are the Chinese. The Chinese know that Western companies are looking to tap either China's one-billion-person marketplace or its vast natural resources. The Chinese, therefore, will use these to attract Western companies to bid on large projects. They will tell the Western company that their bid looks good, but they need additional information before they can award them the contract. Some of the additional information may include trips to the US for training at the Western company's expense. This is the bait and the reward because the Chinese have, for the most part, already decided who would win the contract. These trips are just to take advantage of what the other

Western companies will pay to stay in the bidding process.

In China, Western companies need to be realistic when evaluating their chances at winning large government contracts and know they cannot rely on the encouragement they receive from their Chinese counterpart. The Cultural Translator needs to evaluate the Chinese needs and make sure that they can really meet the Chinese priorities and that the Cultural Translator has established *mianzi* and *guanxi* with his/her counterpart. At the negotiation table, the Cultural Translator also needs to remember that pigs get slaughtered.

11. Victory is determined before the battle begins

The battle should be well planned before it begins, including a contingency plan for each possible mis-chance. The Chinese negotiators thoroughly plan each negotiation before it ever begins; they know exactly where they want to be at the end of the negotiation process and with whom. They will enter into negotiations with companies to whom they never intend to award a contract. That is why it is imperative to understand their cultural traits and their business strategies first before trying to negotiate.

20. The necessity for espionage

Sun-Tzu said, "Armies remain locked in a standoff for years to fight for victory on a single day, yet [generals] begrudge bestowing ranks and emoluments of one hundred pieces of gold and therefore don't know the enemy's situation. This is the ultimate inhumanity. Such a person is not a general for the people, an assistant for a ruler or the arbiter of victory" (Sawyer 1991:231).

To the Chinese business negotiator this means they will try to obtain information on the Western company and on their negotiating team, information that they will be able to utilize during the negotiation process. This will include asking the Western negotiating team questions at the host dinner and later during the casual times when they are buying them drinks. It will also include asking people within their *guanxi* network about the company and its people.

The 36 Strategies

The *36 Strategies* are about 1,500 years old and are comprised of six sections, with each section containing six related strategies. There are several variations of the *36 Strategies*, but the grouping in six appears to be a constant. Due to this grouping of six, it is believed that they originated from the *I Ching,* an ancient belief system associated with the duality of the Yin and the Yang. The number six is significant in the *I Ching*, and the number is associated with deceit among the Chinese (Chu 1995).

These strategies were utilized by some of the great military strategists, including Sun-Tzu and Lin Chin. The *I Ching* relies on the ever-changing Yin and Yang, and the *36 Strategies* refer to methods for manipulating specific manifestations of the universal duality to one's strategic advantage.

The following is a list of the *36 Strategies* that has been taken directly from Chu's (1991) book, *The Asian Mind Game.*

36 STRATEGIES

1. Deceive the sky and cross the ocean.

2. Surrounding Wei to rescue Zao.

3. Borrow Another's hand to kill.

4. Make your enemy work while you wait at leisure.

5. Use the opportunity offered by a fire to rob others.

6. Display your forces in the east and attack in the west.

7. *Create something from nothing.*

8. Secretly utilize the Chen Chang Passage.

9. Watch the fire burning across the river.

10. Knife hidden under the smiling *mianzi*.

11. The plum tree sacrifices for the peach tree.

12. Walk the sheep home, just because it is there.

13. Disturb the snake by hitting the grass.

14. Borrow another's body to return the soul.

15. Entice the tiger to leave the mountain.

16. In order to capture, one must get loose.

17. Trade a brick for a piece of jade.

18. Defeat the enemy by capturing their chief.

19. Remove the firewood under the cooking pot.

20. *The guest becomes the host.*

21. The golden cricket sheds its shell.

22. Accuse others of murder by moving the corpse.

23. Kill the rooster to frighten the monkey.

24. *Steal the dragon and replace it with the phoenix.*

25. Attack when near, befriend when distant.

26. *The hidden message.*

27. Pretend to be a grip in order to eat the tiger.

28. Cross the river and destroy the bridge.

36 STRATEGIES (continued)

29. Be wise by play the fool.

30. Provoke strong emotion.

31. The beauty trap.

32. The empty city.

33. Espionage and counterespionage.

34. Mutilate one's body.

35. Chain links.

36. Escape is the best policy.

(Chu 1991:44–75)

The following is a brief explanation of four of the 36 Strategies and their corresponding number on the list.

7. *Create something from nothing.*

This strategy is designed to make the unreal seem real. The Chinese used this in the 1950s during the Korean Conflict. The Americans had a fixed position and the Chinese rattled cans at night to disturb them. At first the American soldiers were alert, but soon became accustom to the cans. Then one night, the Chinese attacked under the cover of a thousand banging cans.

20. *The guest becomes the host.*

During the business negotiations there are times when the delegations need to travel to the foreign country and negotiate in person. This gives the host country an advantage over the guest, because they can create situations that are favorable to them by controlling where the meeting takes place and by controlling the agenda. It is possible for a clever guest, however, to seize some of the host's advantages by manipulating the cultural mindset and turning the situation to their advantage. An example would be for the Western negotiator to manipulate the agenda by exploiting the host's sense of hospitality, saving *mianzi*, and not wanting to create an incident. By doing this the foreign negotiator can place or remove items from a meeting's agenda that they wish to discuss or not discuss with their host.

24. Steal the dragon and replace it with the phoenix.

This strategy is to give the illusion of a good deal when in reality the deal is not that good. In America, this strategy is known as "bait and switch." This will occur during the negotiation process as the Chinese agree to certain terms or conditions of a contract, but then replace them with something else (generally of lesser quality) during the implementation phase of the contract. This is generally resolved during the post-negotiation process, which, in China, has been dubbed, the post-negotiation negotiations.

26. The hidden message.

The Chinese don't like direct confrontation because it goes against the four cultural complexes; therefore they use indirect criticism to address situations that need attention. They understand what these criticisms are when they are used and how to address them. Foreigners, on the other hand, are not, and can miss a casual hint or misinterpret a story. Foreigners need to be active listeners when dealing with the Chinese because they will not directly address some-thing that is unpleasant. Instead, they will tactfully address it indirectly by dropping hints.

The PRC's Tactics

The purpose of this section is to discuss the ways the Chinese will use deception, time, technology, and culture to achieve an economic advantage during the negotiation process.

As the previous section pointed out, deception plays an important part during the negotiation process. One of the ways that the Chinese negotiators use deception is to gather intelligence on their potential JV partner. The purpose for the intelligence-gathering on the foreign company is to see if they are going to make a good long-term strategic partner. The Chinese want to learn four basic pieces of information regarding the foreign company. First, they want to know the true intent and agenda of the foreign company in establishing this IJV. Secondly, does the foreign company have the latest and most compatible technology for the project and are there any problems with the technology? Third, are they willing to transfer the technology and how much capital do they want to invest? Fourth, are the two organizations culturally compatible? The Chinese take the time and expend the energy to gather this intelligence because they need to know if the foreign company has good *mianzi*, because the Chinese negotiators cannot afford to make a deal that will cost them their *mianzi*. Therefore, they will find out everything they can about the foreign company before entering into an IJV with a foreign partner. Once the Chinese have decided that the foreign company will make a good partner, they will be looking for any additional information that will provide them with a strategic advantage during the negotiation process.

The Chinese are the masters of deception, and the deception starts immediately with the friendly mannerisms, the dinners, and the informal social events—where business is discussed in a more casual atmosphere. While they are getting to know the foreign negotiators and appearing to make new friends, they are really conducting serious intelligence-gathering—looking for any information about the company or members of the negotiating team. This information is then analyzed by the entire Chinese negotiating team before their next meeting with the foreign negotiating team. The Cultural Translator needs to understand that the information-gathering process takes place every minute and never stops. "They believe that all business relationships must be established on their terms and that they must be structured to conform to both the laws of the country as well as cultural practices, even when these practices lack any real justification" (De Mente 1989:121-2).

The Chinese will also utilize time to their strategic advantage because they understand that once the negotiation process starts, so does the clock. The Chinese understand that time is on their side when negotiating a deal with the West. They believe the Western negotiators are under pressure to put the deal together quickly, therefore, they will stall by requesting that presentations be given over and over again to people and sometimes the same people. They will also ask lots of questions and even ask the same ones over again. They do this for two reasons. First, they run out the clock, thus putting the foreign negotiators in a time crunch position. They believe that by running down the clock, they are forcing the foreign negotiating team into a situation to make a snap decision. The Chinese are thinking that this time pressure will make the foreign negotiating team willing to make larger sacrifices in order to reach a last-minute deal. Second, they are looking for discrepancies in the presentations, in the answers to questions, and in the materials provided. Any discrepancy found will be exploited during the negotiation process.

Additional stalling tactics may include needing to get additional approval from someone who was not able to make the meeting, or finding that there is a problem with the technology, therefore, they will need to examine it further. An example of these types of stalling tactics was discussed in the September issue of *Euromoney* (1997). In one example, the Chinese negotiator stated that according to the company, Motorola was working within Thailand, there was a problem with a specific part of Motorola's technology. In this case, the approach did not work to the Chinese advantage because the Motorola negotiator understood their tactics and *mianzi*. The Motorola negotiator did not agree or disagree when the Chinese official made the comment. The Motorola negotiator later called their Thailand office to check on this specific situation and found it to be false. Later, he met with the same Chinese negotiator for a casual meeting where this topic came up again. The Motorola negotiator informed his Chinese counterpart that there was not a problem with the technology in Thailand as he had indicated in the meeting. He then gave him the phone number in Thailand for him to call if he wished to confirm the situation. He then added that he did not want to say anything during the meeting earlier in the day because he did not want to embarrass the Chinese negotiator in front of everyone. The Chinese counterpart thanked him for the number and the next day during the meeting, he pushed for the project's approval. The Motorola negotiator saved the Chinese negotiator's *mianzi*, while at the same time earning *mianzi*. He was able to earn *mianzi* because he respected their culture. He was able to obtain a strategic advantage by understanding their mindset, which enabled him to manipulate the situation to his strategic advantage.

It is important to note that not all delays are stalling tactics. One case I encountered involved one of the largest shipbuilders in China who had established an IJV with a US company based in Kansas. The situation was that the Chinese had to keep delaying various aspects of the IJV due to land negotiations with the farmers. Farmers, who operate in a co-op type arrangement, were currently using the land the Chinese shipbuilder needed to build their new IJV. The Chinese negotiators met with the farmers to negotiate for the right to use the land. Then the farmers sent their representatives to meet with the Chinese negotiators. At each meeting the representatives would settle on a deal and go home to have the all the farmers approve the deal, but that did not happen. Each time the farmers wanted more money, more benefits, which, in the end, included the building of a new school. Even after the company had settled the deal with the farmers, they still had to meet with the local officials to negotiate a lease for the land.

This type of land negotiation situation may appear too many Americans to be a stalling tactic because purchasing land in the US is generally a simple process. In China, however, the land belongs to the people (i.e., to the local authority), but whoever is using the land at the time, especially farmers, have the first rights to that land. The Chinese company, which is a large SOE, had to negotiate with the farmers for the *right* to use the land. Then they had to take this agreement, along with a request for the lease of the land, to the local authorities. The situation did not get out of control because the Chinese company had a good relationship with the American company, which made this process much easier.

The Chinese negotiators will also use cultural misunderstandings as another negotiation tactic. The Chinese will try to manipulate some situation as an insult in China, which would cause an official to loss *mianzi* with his team. They will either raise the issue directly or they will have a lower-ranking official talk to someone on the foreign negotiation team who appears eager to close the deal. The Chinese negotiator will inform the foreign negotiator of the alleged insult and explain to him/her that this Chinese official is very upset about the situation. The Chinese negotiator will also explain that the insulted Chinese negotiator has good *guanxi* or connections and that the deal will not happen unless the Chinese official is able to regain his *mianzi* by closing the deal under certain conditions that favor the Chinese position (De Mente 1989).

All these strategies and tactics are utilized by the Chinese negotiators with the goal of ensuring that they find the best possible partner and the best possible deal. During this entire process, the Chinese will never take their eyes off the end of the game, which is to have a successful IJV on *their* terms.

The Cultural Translator needs to understand that a successful IJV is not just because a contract has been signed. In China, a signed contract does not mean a settled business agreement. On the contrary, to the Chinese, a signed contract is not the end, but the beginning of a relationship that naturally changes from one day to the next and has to be reevaluated and renegotiated on an ongoing basis. This is why they will use these strategies and tactics; it allows them time to get to know their future business partners. This process ensures that their new partners will have good *mianzi* before they make a deal, because once the deal is signed, then the real negotiations begin in what are called the post-negotiation negotiations (De Mente 1989).

Post-Negotiation Negotiations

Another negotiation strategy and tactic is to agree on principles, get the contract signed, and then renegotiate the situation during the implementation process. This tactic has been called the post-negotiation negotiations and is part of the, steal the dragon, leave the phoenix strategy, from the 36 Strategies. One reason why this tactic occurs has to do with the Chinese view of a contract. The Chinese view the contract as a business agreement, not as a legal document; therefore as the business environment

163

changes, so can the obligations of the contract. This is not to say that the Chinese don't honor their contracts or obligations, because they often do, but there are also cases where they did not honor various types of obligations for various reasons.

A case in point happened to the Swedish multinational Ericsson, when the Chinese refused to place the Swedish managing director of the IJV in a Western-standard of housing, as outlined in the contract. The Chinese refused to supply the Western-standard of housing for two reasons. One, the annual cost was about US $70,000, which is equal to about 200 Chinese yearly salaries. The second reason was that it was a much nicer residence than the other Chinese directors were getting for doing the same job at the same IJV. Due to these reasons, this specific point of the contract was re-negotiated (Ghauri N.d.).

Any foreign company doing business in China needs to understand that to the Chinese, their priorities are the only priorities that really matter. In this case, it was obtaining Ericsson's technology, which they were able to do by renegotiating this particular point. The point, however, is that the Chinese were able to obtain the technology without paying full price.

Foreign Company's Strategies and Tactics

Foreign companies also need to employ a combination of strategies and tactics to ensure that their goal of a successful IJV is achieved. This section will discuss how foreign companies can achieve a strategic advantage during the negotiation process by

examining the PRC's economic priorities and by manipulating the four cultural complexes.

The PRC's Priorities

A foreign company's negotiation priorities should
be centered on developing a strategic advantage during the negotiation process. They will not be able to
accomplish this unless they understand what the
CA's and local authority's priorities are in attracting
Foreign Direct Investment (FDI).

The first priority of the CA is to make China economically self-relent. To accomplish this, Deng Xiaoping, in 1975, outlined his plan for what he called
the Four Modernizations: Agriculture, Industry, Science and Technology, and National Defense. Deng
and the CA believed that by modernizing these areas, China would be able to achieve and maintain its
self-reliance. However, to reach this level of self-
reliance, Deng and the CA understood that they
would first need assistance from others, including
Western countries and companies, in raising the
amount of Foreign Direct Investment (FDI) needed
to modernize China. Therefore, the CA made FDI in
the form of cash, technology, capital equipment, and
modern management techniques their top priorities
(Chen 1997a).

As Table 5.3 indicates, the CA has been very successful in raising FDI, making China the second-
largest recipient of FDI behind the United States;
however, they have not been able to obtain the capital equipment and technology that they are seeking.
Table 5.1 shows that that the manufacturing and real estate sectors of the economy have received respectively 56.67 percent and 28.54 percent of the to-

tal FDI raised between 1983 and 1995 (Chen 1997b). These numbers are significant because these two segments of the economy absorbed 85.21 percent of the total FDI, which leaves less than 15 percent of the total FDI for the CA's other priorities, such as agriculture, and science and technology. Clearly the CA has been successful in raising FDI; however it is also clear that the CA has been finding it difficult to meet all of their priorities.

This becomes clearer with an examination of Table 5.2, which lists an industry breakdown of the Foreign-Funded Enterprises (FFEs) within the manufacturing sector. At a quick glance, the Electronics and Telecommunications equipment manufacturing industry, which is a technology-intensive industry and a high priority of the CA, received 11.29 percent of the total FFE funding. While the textile industry, a labor-intensive industry and not a high priority of the CA, received 8.59 percent of the total FFE funding. It appears that the Electronics and Telecommunications equipment industry has received the largest share of the FFEs funding, which it has. However, when the manufacturing sector is divided into labor-, capital-, and technology-intensive groups, the implications of those numbers become clear. The labor-intensive segment[5] of all the manufacturing industries accounts for 50.42 percent of the total FFE funding, while the capital-[6] and technology-

---

[5] Labor-intensive: Food processing, Food manufacturing, Textiles, Clothing & other fiber products, Leather & Fur products, Timber processing, Furniture, Paper & Paper products, Printing, Cultural, Education & Sports goods, Rubber products, Plastic products, Non-metal minerals products, and Other.

[6] Capital-intensive: Beverage manufacturing, Tobacco processing, Petroleum refining & Coking, Chemical materials & products, Chemical fibers, Ferrous metal smelting & pressing, Non-ferrous metal smelting & pressing, and Transport equipment.

intensive[7] sectors only received 22.73 and 26.85 percent respectively. This is important because it means that foreign companies are investing in their priorities, which is the labor-intensive industry and not the CA's priorities of capital- and technology-intensive industries. Keep in mind that the CA is looking to the capital- and technology-intensive industries to provide China the tools it will need to become self-reliant.

Another factor that is important to understand is China's geographic priorities for attracting FDI. As Table 5.3 illustrates, there is an enormous amount of FDI entering China. In the beginning the FDI was concentrated in the four SEZs located in the Guangdong and Fujian regions. As the CA was able to adjust their policies, taxes and incentives to meet the requirements of the foreign companies, they allowed the coastal areas to start offering similar incentives to attract FDI. As figure 5.1 illustrates, this has been a successful program. Then, to attract FDI to other geographic areas, the CA again changed its geographic priorities for FDI by lowering the incentives that the coastal areas can offer and increasing the offers from other areas. This has also proved to be a successful arrangement as figure 5.2 illustrates.

The CA has been able to attract FDI to different regions of China by adjusting the incentives that various regions can offer. It makes these adjustments to meet the current economic and political demands of the various regions. An example of this can be seen in the inner regions. The CA offers for-

---

[7] Technology-intensive: Medical & Pharmaceutical products, General machinery, Special machinery, Electrical machinery & equipment, Electronics & Telecommunication equipment, and Instruments & Meters.

eign companies the option of selling 100 percent of their products within the local market, while the coastal areas are limited to 30 percent. They also offer various types of income tax incentives as well.

The CA can make these incentive adjustments because the approval process for FDI is centrally controlled. Therefore, it is easy to discover what the national priorities are, but it can be difficult to pinpoint what the CA's specific priorities are because they change according to the economic situations in the given regions. In addition, the local authorities, whose approval is required for almost every venture except those in the SEZs or involving a selected few SOEs, have their own sets of priorities.

This is one of the reasons why *guanxi* is needed in China: to gather intelligence. The Chinese negotiators will know the specific priorities regarding each IJV, but they will generally not disclose those priorities to the foreign company. They will not disclose that information because they believe it would give the foreign company a strategic advantage during the negotiation process. Therefore, one job of the Cultural Translator is to find out what these priorities are.

Table 5.1

The Distribution of Contracted FDI Inflows in China by Industry Between 1983 and 1995 (percent)

(Source: Chen 1997:10)

Year	Agri culture	Manu- facture	Con struc tion	Tran. & Tele.	Com merce	Real Estate	Health Edu. & Sci.	Others
1983	0.93	66.89	2.96	3.13	2.05	4.95	19.10	0.00
1984	2.74	21.97	2.71	2.92	3.83	33.46	32.37	0.00
1985	1.99	37.65	2.09	1.67	8.31	35.85	0.99	11.45
1986	3.13	37.07	1.58	1.00	3.01	48.56	1.72	3.92
1987	3.98	52.34	1.27	0.38	0.68	34.06	0.61	6.69
1988	4.08	77.61	1.92	1.47	1.04	8.56	0.92	4.40
1989	2.10	84.47	1.06	0.83	1.07	8.32	0.74	1.40
1990	1.98	85.07	2.59	0.52	1.53	6.48	1.07	0.76
1991	1.82	80.95	1.08	0.80	1.41	12.11	1.12	0.71
1992	1.26	56.53	3.13	2.63	2.46	30.78	0.94	2.27
1993	1.09	45.12	3.46	1.36	4.11	39.09	1.36	3.40
1994	1.18	53.31	2.88	2.44	4.72	28.72	3.45	3.30
1995	1.90	67.54	2.10	1.86	3.75	19.54	1.60	1.71
Total	1.52	56.67	2.74	1.85	3.67	28.54	2.15	2.85

Table 5.2

The Percentage of Industrial Distribution of FFEs and DOEs in Manufacturing from 1983 to 1995

Industry	FFD	DE
Food processing	4.55	4.16
Food manufacturing	3.28	1.63
Beverage manufacturing	3.65	2.55
Tobacco processing	0.10	2.46
Textile	8.59	8.75
Clothing & other fiber products	5.01	1.29
Leather & Fur products	3.34	0.91
Timber processing	1.30	0.67
Furniture	0.77	0.33
Paper & Paper products	2.21	2.10
Printing	1.14	0.97
Cultural, Education & Sports goods	1.33	0.42
Petroleum refining & Coking	0.26	3.70
Chemical materials & products	5.38	8.82
Medical & Pharmaceutical products	2.29	2.24
Chemical fiber	1.57	2.09
Rubber products	1.59	1.12
Plastic products	4.06	1.62
Non-metal mineral products	6.55	7.88
Ferrous metal smelting & pressing	2.53	12.38
Non-ferrous metal smelting & processing	1.61	2.98
Metal products	4.77	2.71
General machinery	4.03	6.18
Special machinery	1.77	4.67
Transportation equipment	7.62	7.15
Electrical machinery & equipment	6.05	4.63
Electronics & Telecom. Equipment	11.29	3.33
Instruments & Meters	1.43	1.08
Others	1.93	0.88
Total	**100**	**100**

(Source: Chen 1997a:10)

Table 5.3

FDI Inflows into China's Host Provinces
1983–1995

Province	'83–'88	'89	'90	'91	'92	'93	'94	'95	Total
Beijing	495	213	176	148	205	380	762	584	2963
Tianjin	163	21	23	80	63	299	564	822	2035
Hebei	25	29	28	34	66	226	291	296	995
Shanxi	9.1	7	2	2	32	49	18	35	154
Inner Mongol.	11	3	7	1	3	49	22	31	127
Liaoning	174	84	162	219	303	729	800	770	3241
Jilin	17	7	11	19	44	157	134	221	610
Heilongjiang	64	38	18	13	42	132	193	279	779
Shanghai	376	280	110	88	290	1801	1374	1564	5883
Jiangsu	169	84	84	133	859	1621	2091	2806	7847
Zhejiang	68	36	31	56	141	588	639	680	2239
Anhui	28	6	9	6	32	147	206	261	695
Fujian	189	231	202	285	836	1635	2063	2186	7627
Jiangxi	15	6	5	12	59	119	145	156	517
Shandong	130	109	117	131	589	1068	1418	1454	5016
Henan	59	31	7	23	31	174	215	259	799
Hubei	39	19	20	28	119	308	334	338	1205
Hunan	19	15	9	15	78	249	184	274	843
Guangdong	1904	879	998	1175	2173	4308	5257	5546	22240
Guangxi	69	35	22	19	107	504	465	364	1576
Hainan	138	71	65	107	266	403	510	574	2134
Sichuan	63	9	15	49	66	326	512	293	1333
Guizhou	12	8	7	9	12	24	35	31	138
Yunnan	12	5	5	2	17	55	36	53	185
Tibet	2	0	0	0	0	0	0	0	2
Sichuan	143	65	30	19	27	134	133	175	726
Gansu	5.2	0	1	3	0.2	7	49	35	100
Qinghai	0.4	0	0	0	0.4	2	1.3	0.9	7
Ningxia	0.5	0.7	0.2	0.1	2	7	4	2.1	17
Xinjiang	22	0.6	3	0.1	0	30	27	30	112
Total	4422	2292	2167	2676	6463	15531	18482	20120	72145

(Source: Chen 1997c:14)

(Millions of US dollars at 1980 constant prices)

Figure 5.1

The Distribution of Accumulated FDI in China from 1984 to 1991

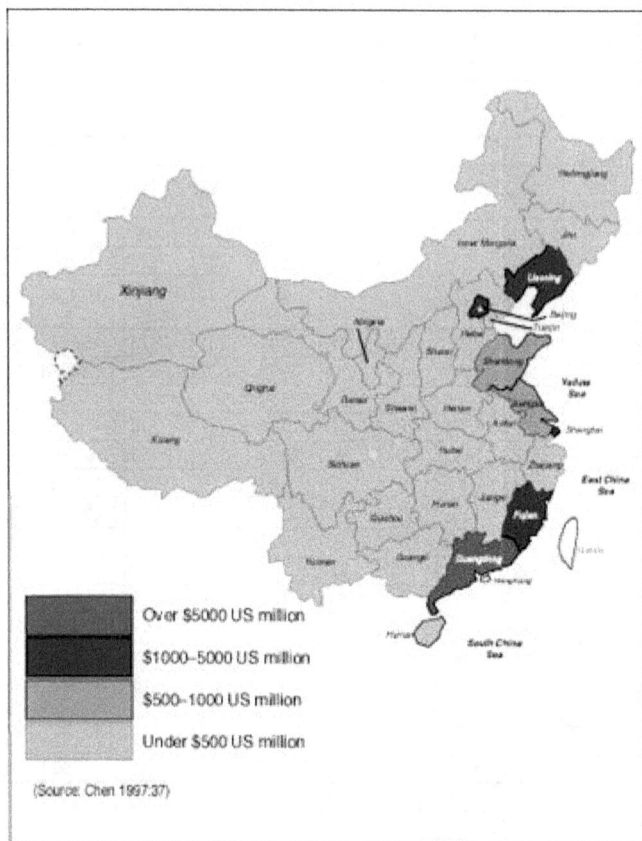

Over $5000 US million

$1000–5000 US million

$500–1000 US million

Under $500 US million

(Source: Chen 1997:37)

Figure 5.2

The Distribution of Accumulated FDI in China from 1992 to 1995

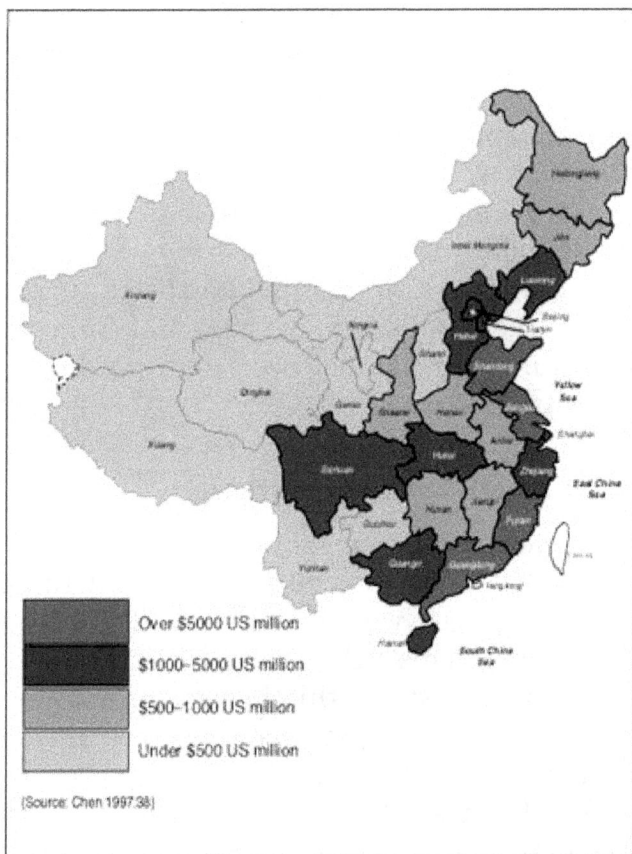

Manipulating the Cultural Mindset

The Chinese negotiators are not the only ones who should be using strategy to achieve a strategic advantage during the negotiation process. The foreign companies must do so as well. However, the foreign negotiators not only need to understand and use Sun-Tzu's *The Art of War* and the *36 Strategies*, they also need to know how to manipulate the Four Cultural Complexes to their advantage. This section will discuss how to manipulate the cultural complexes by showing how a foreigner can obtain *mianzi* and *guanxi* by following *keqi* and *renqing*. However, before discussing how to manipulate the cultural complexes, we need to discuss one aspect of Chinese and Asian culture that has not been addressed, the concept of cultural superiority.

Cultural Superiority

A Chinese Emperor in the 18th Century once said, "Our Celestial Empire possessed all things in prolific abundance...we have no need of the products of outside barbarians" (De Keijzer 1992: 214).

To a certain extent, this holds true today. The concept of culturally superior and inferior groups has not been questioned in Asia, as it has been in the West. The Chinese, Japanese, Koreans, and most of the other groups of people in Southeast Asia have strong feelings regarding the subject of cultural superiority. Asians don't have the same sensitivity to racial issues, as do Americans. They regard an ethnocentric view as natural. To them everything about themselves is superior to everyone else; this includes their culture, their country, their state, town, neighborhood, street, and even their families. Cultural superiority is as much a part of their cultural mindset as anything else. Understanding that this attitude of superiority exists is of vital importance to the Cultural Translator because it influences how the Chinese conduct themselves (Chu 1991).

Therefore, when attempting to manipulate the cultural complexes to achieve a strategic advantage during the negotiation process, it is vital to make sure that the actions taken don't appear condescending or insincere. At all times, there must be a real and natural sense of equality and fellowship building between the negotiating teams. For if there is not, and the Chinese believe that the foreign negotiators are trying to manipulate them or are not sincere in their efforts to build friendship, the Chinese will take it as a loss of *mianzi*. The result will be an act of revenge because that is what *renqing* demands when *mianzi* is lost. That is why this book has stressed the importance using a Cultural Translator to assist foreign companies in their efforts to conduct business internationally.

Manipulating the Cultural Complexes

To achieve a strategic advantage in China, the foreign company and its negotiators need to have *mianzi* to obtain the *guanxi* necessary to get the contracts. This section, therefore, will discuss two methods of gaining *mianzi* and *guanxi*. The first method is the quickest way of gaining *mianzi* and *guanxi,* and that is to utilize the Overseas Chinese and the *taizi*, who are the sons and daughters of the Communist Revolution. The second and the proper way of establishing *mianzi* and *guanxi* are to develop an understanding of the Chinese people and cultivate friendships. With this second method, the foreign company and negotiating team earn their *mianzi* and *guanxi* by following the cultural rules associated with *keqi* and *renqing*.

The Quick Way to Establish Mianzi and Guanxi

As discussed in chapter two, earning *mianzi* and *guanxi* takes time and requires *keqi* and *renqing*. However, there are ways to speed up the process and that is by borrowing (or purchasing) someone else's *mianzi* and *guanxi*. I call this face transference. Western companies use this face transference method from overseas Chinese and the *taizi*, who are the sons and daughters of China's top cadres, as an avenue to the large national projects.

Overseas Chinese

When China first opened its doors in 1979, there was only one official controlled mode of introduction—the Canton Trade Fair. The other and unofficial form of introduction was through overseas Chinese, mainly from Hong Kong. Today, there are countless ways of obtaining a formal introduction to a Chinese company that is actively seeking an IJV with a Western com-pany. However, there are only two ways of obtaining enough *mianzi* and *guanxi* in a short amount of time to be able to bid on the large Chinese projects—though the overseas Chinese or the *taizi*.

Overseas Chinese is a term that refers to all ethnic Chinese that don't live on the mainland within the PRC; therefore, the Chinese in Hong Kong and Taiwan are considered overseas Chinese, as are ethnic Chinese on the mainland of Southeast Asia. Over half of the 40 million plus overseas Chinese in the world can be traced to just two southern provinces in China—Guangdong (across from Hong Kong) and Fujian (across the strait from Taiwan) (Weidenbaum 1996).

The overseas Chinese businesspeople are unusual because, unlike Japanese or Western managers, who go from one international assignment to another, the overseas Chinese tend to immigrate permanently and become involved within their new host culture. They develop close ties to the local governments, speak their new host country's language, and often take local names. In their own homes, however, they are Chinese. They celebrate Chinese holidays, speak Chinese, eat traditional Chinese food, send their children to Chinese schools, and observe other Chinese customs. This ability to live completely in two cultures at the same time has been classified by Geert Hofstede (1984) as bi-culturalism. The term appeals to the overseas Chinese because they are masters at fitting into a new environment. An explanation of their bi-cultural ability stems from the fact that the majority of them never really left China psychologically (Weidenbaum 1996). They maintain their Chinese cultural continuity and identities.

There are about 40 million overseas Chinese in the world, with the largest settlement outside of Asia, about one million, in California (Kotkin 1992). These may or may not seem like impressive numbers, but the economic power they have managed to obtain is impressive. "In 1994, the total assets of the 500 largest public companies in Asia controlled by overseas Chinese exceeded $500 billion" (Weidenbaum 1996:24). Though they own stock in large publicly-owned corporations, they typically consist of cross-holdings of privately-owned, family-run, trade-oriented firms, rather than allowing themselves to become huge publicly-owned manufacturing corporations that are typical in the United States, Japan, and Western Europe (Weidenbaum 1996).

To put their true economic power in perspective, in Thailand, the overseas Chinese make up only 10 percent of the total population, but they control over 80 percent of the market value of listed companies. In Indonesia they make up only about 3.5 percent of the population, but account for about 73 percent of the public capital. Numbers like this are the rule all over Southeast Asia, except for Korea and Japan. The $500 billion stated earlier was for assets of public companies in Asia only. Their real economic might in 1995 was about $2.5 trillion (Kwong 1996).

This economic success does not come without a price, however. They have met with strong discrimination in almost every country, in the forms of racial violence and discriminatory laws.

Due to their bi-cultural ability and economic success, it is no wonder that Westerners flocked to seek the assistance of overseas Chinese in dealing with the PRC. By the end of 1994, HK Chinese had invested about $67.3 billion into the PRC. This is a staggering amount considering that the United States had only invested $6.1 billion, and most of that was from overseas Chinese living in the States.

Their success does not just come from capital; it also comes from their willingness and ability to take risks. They have been successful in China because they are the ones who took the risks and invested at the time when there were no real legal guarantees of property rights, price deregulation, tax laws, or international arbitration. They were not risk free, but they had their *guanxi* to protect their investments.

There are two other reasons why overseas Chinese have been successful. The first is their organizational structure. Most of the businesses are family owned and operated, making decision-making quick and efficient. The other is *guanxi*; they have the connections to local and national governments to implement their quick decisions. Due to their ability to make decisions quickly and to utilize their *guanxi* with each other, they have been able to invest where they wanted around the world without worrying about borders. Due to these factors, Western businesses are seeking their assistance in working with the PRC.

As an example how the overseas Chinese operate, two charts have been utilized from Murray Weidenbaum's (1996) *The Bamboo Network*; figures 5.3 and 5.4 to illustrate their extensive networks.

Figure 5.3:

Important Cross-Holdings of the Charoen Pokphand Group

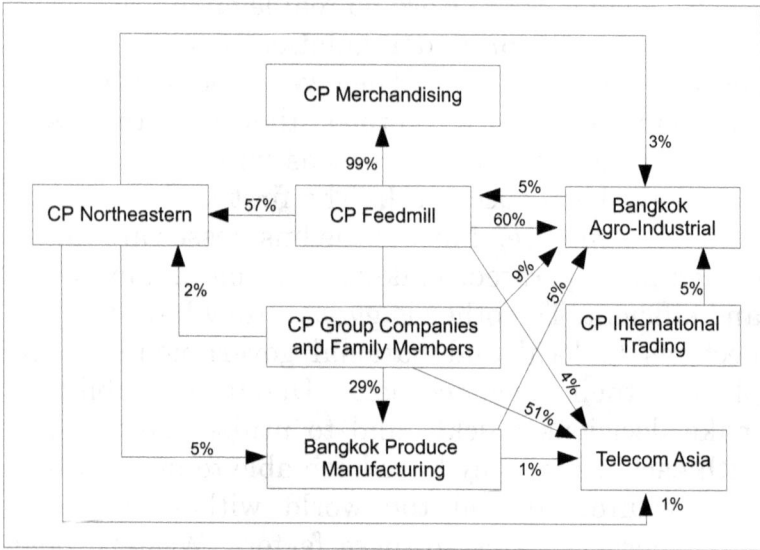

(Source: Weidenbrum 1996:86)

Figure 5.4:

Salim Group Public Company

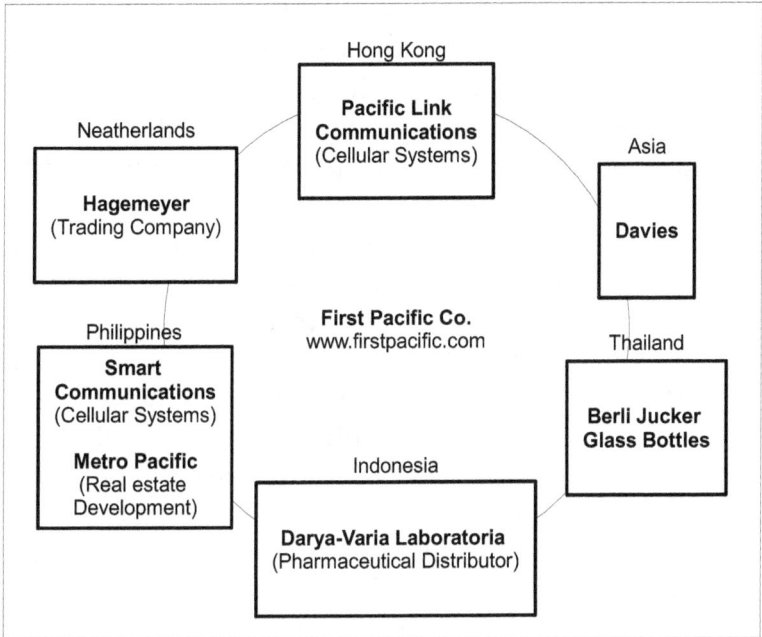

(Source: Weidenbrum 1996:89)

Cultural Continuity

Some foreign companies are hiring overseas Chinese directly, and as consultants, to use their cultural continuity as a strategy to speed up the process, and as a way of manipulating the cultural complexes to their advantage without understanding them. They believe that working through the overseas Chinese, who share a similar culture with the PRC Chinese, are a quick and cheap, route to conducting business in China. However, there is an old Chinese saying, "Do not be afraid of Heaven, do not be afraid of hell, be afraid of a Cantonese speaking Mandarin" (Engholm 1994).

Cultural continuity is defined as "similar cultural traits shared across political boundaries." This section will be addressing the concept of cultural continuity by comparing the cultural traits of the PRC Chinese and those of overseas Chinese. It would appear logical to assume that the two groups share a similar cultural mindset, but it would be wrong to assume that they have similar motivational factors when it comes to how they conduct business negotiations. To discuss this in greater detail, this section will discuss Michael Solt's (1995) study on the "Perceptions about managerial advancement in the People's Republic of China" that was published in *The International Executive*. His study compared management motivational differences between Chinese managers from the mainland (PRC), Hong Kong (HK) and United States (US). These three distinct groups of Chinese share a similar cultural background, but they are not identical. Each group lives in its own unique Socio-cultural setting. For instance, the HK Chinese may look similar to the PRC Chinese, they can speak the same language and, to a certain extent, they have similar values in regard to family, friends, and obligations. However, they grew-up in one of the most capitalistic places on the planet, Hong Kong. While the PRC managers, on the other hand, grew up under communism and lived through the Cultural Revolution. Therefore, the HK managers are not going to make the same managerial decisions as PRC managers due to the differences in their value systems.

Solt pointed out that the PRC managers are pushing national development objectives via SOEs. They do this because the ultimate authority resides with the Central Authority (CA). As a consequence, the Western company is not negotiating only with a Chinese company as it might a peer. They are also negotiating with the bureaucrats within the CA. As the "political arena" section discussed, authority hierarchies within the CA are not clear and identifying the real decision-makers is often difficult. In contrast, in Hong Kong, with its liberal government (even with the hand-over back to the PRC) and the predominance of private firms pushing profit motives, authority hierarchies are clear and decision-makers are easily identified. The differences between their incentives are that the PRC managers have broad national incentives for taking risks with possible negative outcomes that might lead to penalties for themselves. Hong Kong managers, however, are willing to accept high risks because they can expect to share in the economic benefits predicted.

Solt also compared the strategies and ethical behavior of US managers and HK managers, and found that US managers' preferred more individualistic, open job tactics (i.e., talking to the boss in regard to a promotion), and viewed ethical behavior as absolute. While Hong Kong managers preferred more collectivist and behind-the-scenes job activities (i.e., talking to others and having them discuss the promotion with the Chinese manager's boss) and viewed ethical behavior as situation dependent.

An example of this difference in ethical behavior can be seen in these managers' strategies for career advancement. Solt's research found that US managers, who are from an individualistic, low power-distance culture, prefer overt advancement tactics that showcase their individual talents (Solt 1995:421). While Hong Kong and PRC managers preferred a similar approach involving covert tactics through their guangxi network of family and close friends. They share this similar approach because of their similar heritage and collectivist, high power-distance culture and Confucian values (Solt 1995:421). Both the PRC and HK managers view this form of information control/networking tactics as more ethical than do US managers because there is a higher likelihood of success with low personal risk.

It is this similar culture, based on Confucian values and teachings that emphasize social hierarchy, a respect for tradition, an ordering of relationships by status, and a desire to save *mianzi*, that gives PRC and Hong Kong managers their cultural continuity and separates them from US managers.

This cultural continuity between HK and PRC managers has its limits, due to their different cultural situations. The PRC managers are from an autocratic Communist state that is stable, with national development objectives pushed by government organizations. While HK managers are the products of liberal colonialism with an uncertain future in which private companies strive for profit objectives.

This difference can be observed in their uses of personal contacts, an attribute that both believe to be ethical in obtaining advancement. The use of personal contacts appears to be stronger in HK managers than with the PRC managers because the actual decision-makers with the PRC are not typically clear, unlike in HK, which maintains a corporate culture with individual accountability. Due to the uncertain authority hierarchy, the PRC manager might view the use of personal contacts in gathering information on a rival as less ethical, in spreading rumors as more risky, and in blackmailing as less likely. Another reason for this line of thinking by PRC managers is that their superiors may be political appointees who are frequently reassigned, making survival a top priority.

Solt found that potential penalties weigh heavy on PRC managers' minds when they calculate what risky or acceptable behavior is. While the HK managers weighed the benefits and potential rewards. This difference in their cultural continuity does not go unnoticed among themselves. HK managers view PRC man-agers as lazy and apathetic, while PRC managers think that HK managers are arrogant and contemptuous and have exaggerated self-importance.

Overseas Chinese do share the same four cultural complexes and business strategies as mainland Chinese; however, Solt's study has also indicated that their relevant political, legal, and economic backgrounds strongly influence how they make and rationalize their decisions. A professionally-trained Cultural Translator can help a negotiator understand and deal with these differences.

Taizi:
The Sons and Daughters of China's Top Cadres

The overseas Chinese are not the only ones with impressive *guanxi* in the PRC. The *taizi* are the sons and daughters of China's communist revolutionaries who have ascended to the tops of companies and are the new rich. There is an old saying, "When a man becomes an official, his wife, children, dogs, cats, and even chickens fly up to heaven. When he falls, they fall with him" (Malhotra 1995:1).

The *taizi* are utilizing their family's good *mianzi* and *guanxi* for personal political advancement and profit. A typical example would be Wang Jun, the son of the late Vice President and leftist party stalwart Wang Zhen. Wang Jun is the executive directive director and general manager of China International Trust & Investment Corp. (CITIC), the country's biggest investment company. He is also president of arms-trading company Poly Technologies, Inc., a PLA enterprise affiliated with CITIC. According to the Malhotra (1995), Wang is just a connection man, with no education and no other contribution.

Wang Jun is not alone; there are about 2500 to 3000 relatives of top Communist Party members, who are considered *taizi*. The *taizi* have secured their way of life and jobs through their father's *guanxi*. There are those *taizi* who don't fit the stereotype, they are educated professionals, and they will be essential to China's development. The *taizi* are the elite, and China needs their skills, according to one European diplomat. They are involved in everything, and it would be difficult to find a major project in which they are not involved. The *taizi* have also taken steps in recent years to secure their reigns and their inheritance of the CCP by exploiting their *guanxi* to take control of the country's new market economy and become dollar millionaires, something their fathers would not have wanted to happen, considering they fought the Nationalist or KMT (Kuonimtang) during the Civil War because of corruption. "Now, half a century later, it is even worse. Once again, a few families control both government and business" (Malhotra 1995). In 1993, Deng's family had an interest in 14 publicly listed companies in Hong Kong, which had a book value of more than $2 billion (Malhotra 1995).

There is an estimate that over 2800 of the *taizi* hold top military and government jobs and about 900 of them operate international trading companies. "At Poly Technologies, marshal Ye Jianying's son, Ye Xuanlian, is a manager. Wang Xiaochao, former President Yang Shangkun's son-in-law, and Col He Ping, a son-in-law of Deng Xiaoping, are former general managers. Yang Li, Yang's daughter, and Wang Zihua, son-in-law of former General Secretary Zhao Ziyang, also have worked for Poly Technologies. The president of another PLA enterprise, Kaili Corp., is Marshal Ye's son Ye Xuanning. At manufacturer Great Wall Computer Co. in Beijing, the general manager is Wang Zhi, Wang Jun's youngest brother. In Hong Kong, CITIC's hugely successful private vehicle, CITIC Hong Kong, is headed by Larry Yung, the son of former CITIC boss and current Vice President Rong Yiren" (Malhotra 1995:1).

Driving the *taizi* is a lifestyle like the one achieved by Larry Yung. He purchased the late British Prime Minister Harold Macmillan home, a 335-hectare country estate and a 14-bedroom mansion in England. He owns three Mercedes-Benzes and a Porsche. This is not excess in their eyes, most of them believe they are entitled to this life style because what happened to their parents during the

Cultural Revolution, being purged and sent to re-education camps. To them this is compensation.

This excess is not going unnoticed by the top CCP officials, who understand that they have allowed this to happen. Jiang is trying to slow this type of excess and his first real step in this direction came during the 14 Party Congress in 1992 when none of the *taizi* were promoted to senior positions.

The future role of the *taizi* in China will be primarily one connected to *guanxi*. In the US, "Chen Weili, daughter of top conservative official Chen Yun, and Zhang Xiabin, son of former Public Health Minister Cui Yueli, studied at Stanford University in California before they joined with others to found China Venturetech Investment Corp., a major venture capital investment company backed by government agencies. Another son of Deng Xiaoping, Deng Zhifang, studied at the University of Rochester in New York and later became chairman of property developer Shanghai Grand Development Co. Deng Zhifang's son was born in the US, which under American law entitles him to citizenship" (Malhotra 1995:1).

The problem with *taizi* is that they are just connections or a method of achieving an introduction to a big project. Often they can also offer much needed government support or backing, but they cannot solve the cultural problems associated with joint venture failures. This is the same problem with overseas Chinese. They offer protection from the CCP, the State, and the local officials but they cannot manage a joint venture. A Cultural Translator can help to bridge the cultural gap and turn the joint venture into a moneymaker.

Today the PRC has developed a political organizational structure to work with foreigners; the PRC no longer needs to rely on the overseas Chinese for introductions to foreign companies. The pride issue is very strong, the PRC managers are showing that they don't need the overseas Chinese to work with the foreign companies because they now have the experience and knowledge to work with them one on one.

Another problem concerning the use of HK as business partners or negotiators concerns their past dealings with their PRC counterparts. The overseas Chinese from HK have been dealing with the PRC since the open door policy began and there is no doubt that some of the deals favored HK more than the PRC. This has created a tendency to mistrust the integrity and reliability of the HK managers (Engholm 1994).

The Proper Way of Establishing
Mianzi and *Guanxi*

As discussed in chapter two, the proper way to establish *mianzi* and *guanxi* is by establishing real friendships in China. This is not going to be an easy task due to the clannishness and conformity of Chinese culture. Clannishness and conformity have their origins in the strong family unity and social conformity values found in the various Chinese philosophies: Buddhism, Taoism, and Confucian thought. Though these concepts have been a part of Chinese culture for millennia, it was the harsh treatment during the Cultural Revolution that really reinforced the absolute dependence upon and necessity of *mianzi* and *guanxi* in the mindsets of the younger generations. This section therefore will examine how to establish *mianzi* and *guanxi* through lobbying, community involvement, and third parties.

One type of lobbying that needs to be conducted on both a national and local level is through advertisements in trade journals. These advertisements need to be in national trade journals explaining who the foreign company is, what it does, where it is located, and what it has done in the past for other customers. The idea behind this general advertisement is to show that the foreign company is financially strong and stable. Then when trying to win a specific contract, the foreign company needs to tailor its advertisements more specifically to that project. Chinese officials are more willing to listen to foreign companies if they also support these publications and stay involved in China when there is not a big contract on the table. This is part of the relationship building that is required.

Another type of lobbying that needs to take place involves personal contacts with Chinese officials at both local and national levels. This type of lobbying needs to be conducted nationally as well as locally because local officials influence the national contracts. This type of lobbying requires the foreign company's officials to personally meet with and establish a good relationship with their Chinese counterparts. This will include taking the officials out to informal, "just getting to know you" dinners and activities. The foreign company's official should make a real effort to get to know as much as they can about the Chinese officials' families, including how many children they have, their birthdays, ages and grades. The point here is to get to know them on a personal level, not just on a professional one. Part of this effort will include becoming involved with the community, such as sponsoring community events. This is not a new concept. Companies in America sponsor sporting events, parks, zoos, as well as hospitals and other programs all the time. Why would it be any different in China?

Targeted lobbying will also need to be utilized when there is an actual contract in the balance. This is lobbying is focused on specific individuals involved in the decision-making process for a specific contract. This lobbying will need to include paying for inspection trips of the foreign company's home-country head-quarters and other facilities. These inspection trips will need to include both national and some local officials. The purpose of this journey is not just a free trip, but to ensure the foreign company will be able to fulfill the contract, because if the contract or IJV fails, then they lose *mianzi*. Therefore, they will go to extensive ends to make sure the foreign company has good *mianzi* and will not cause them to lose *mianzi*.

Such lobbying efforts may appear to be a serious waste of time and money, but they are not. Their true purpose is to show that the foreign company supports China. It also puts the foreign company's name in front of Chinese officials. Therefore, if they all know this particular foreign company from meeting with its officials, seeing its advertisement in their Chinese journals, they will know if they have good *mianzi* or not. The Chinese officials will also know if the foreign company is well liked by local and national officials. With these factors working for the foreign company, the chances of winning the contract become much greater due their own *mianzi* and *guanxi* achieved through their personal contacts and lobbying efforts. A strategic advantage has been achieved.

Formal introductions, however, can sometimes be difficult to obtain due to the clannishness of Chinese culture. Because of this, it is sometimes necessary to use a third party as a means of achieving formal introduction.

Third parties are often employed to facilitate a formal mode of introductions. However, as the section on overseas Chinese and *taizi* indicated, a third party's *guanxi* can influence the decision-making process. The third party can be any person or organization that already has good *mianzi* in China, such as a bank, a trading company or another company. Their *guanxi* can especially be of great assistance in gaining introductions to the correct officials. The West, as discussed earlier, utilized the overseas Chinese living in Hong Kong because the HK Chinese have a similar cultural background and speak the language of the PRC. However, a foreign company should not assume that a common cultural link will overcome the regional loyalties and idiosyncrasies of the various parts of China. One problem is the view of the PRC of people from Hong Kong. Due to the friction between the PRC and HK managers, a foreign company going into China in partnership with an HK-based company, may lose some of its own *mianzi*. The PRC managers may think that the company is not big or strong enough to enter China on its own (Engholm 1994). It is also important to remember when relying on a third party, the foreign company's future is now tied to that relationship. It is like the old Chinese saying, when they fall, they all fall with them.

Obtaining *guanxi* is complicated because it is based on *mianzi* and *renqing*. Therefore there is no 'golden' rule for establishing *guanxi*. In China, business relationships often originate in an unorthodox manner because of China's provincial, fiefdom-like organizational structure that puts a premium on personal connections (Engholm 1994). The foreign company helps a Chinese company in trouble, and in return the Chinese company helps the foreign company when it is in trouble. That is what *guanxi* is about, helping each other out.

The *guanxi* of the overseas Chinese was utilized by the West throughout the 1980s as a means of establishing a network of business connections and of creating a good reputation among Chinese customers. Many companies chose Hong Kong as their Asia headquarters, due to the *guanxi* networks that were available through the overseas Chinese and because Hong Kong was still a British colony until 1997. However, most of the smaller companies that were just selling their products in China maintained their offices in their respective countries, not in Hong Kong. This did pose some problems, mainly that the company was isolated from its customers and away from new developments within the Chinese business community (Engholm 1994).

Companies may consider opening an office in China to assist in establishing *guanxi* and locating a good Chinese partner. The cost of opening an office in China can be staggering. The estimates run from $250,000 to over $300,000 a year for office space and placing an expatriate in Beijing or Shanghai. For the same cost, a company could send a small team to China once a month for the whole year at $20,000 a trip. There are other, more cost-effective ways of establishing *guanxi* and locating potential business partners than opening an office. One way is through a third party, such as the US Chamber of Commerce, the Chinese Consulate business office, or even a US Consulate business officer in China (Engholm 1994).

When establishing *guanxi*, foreign companies need to be careful and follow the rules of *renqing* because *guanxi* is a reciprocal process. If they do a favor for someone, they expect that person to do a favor for them in return. *Mianzi* ensures that the favor will be returned, even if they don't want to do the favor. Failure to fulfill a *guanxi* obligation will result in being blacklisted from the *guanxi* network, losing *mianzi*, and suffering an act of revenge against the person who failed to fulfill the cultural obligation (Weidenbaum 1996). The network of support created by *guanxi* is very strong, but it is not free. *Renqing* is why *guanxi* works.

The cultural rules surround *keqi* and *renqing* are why *mianzi* and *guanxi* work in Chinese culture, but foreigners entering Chinese culture are not tied to these same cultural obligations. Therefore, the Chinese have learned to protect their *mianzi* by first associating with foreigners in a ritual setting. This allows both parties to interact within a controlled environment where the rules of interaction are set.

It is not surprising that rituals also play an important part in business, dominating meetings, banquets, and all the other forms of social and business interactions. Rituals are stressed in Buddhism and Confucius thought as a means of maintaining order and stability. Rituals create an air of sincerity in the midst of serious doubts about whether business can be conducted between the two groups and, most importantly, the formal structure allows individuals to be polite and maintain *mianzi.*

Chinese rituals are not to be taken lightly or to be considered a waste of time. Experience dictates that rituals must never be ignored, whether by a new-comer or by an old China hand, because this could cause the person to lose m*ianzi.* There are also other practical reasons for maintaining the integrity of the rituals and protocols. In China, the formal meeting of both delegations at a host party also has another practical purpose, which is to collect information on the foreign company about their priorities, goals, plans, and technology.

The Chinese will take advantage of this ritual to ask questions and take notes. They will later combine their notes and find out what they have learned about the visiting delegation, their true purpose, what technology they have to offer, and what type of venture they are planning. Any weaknesses they can find will also be exploited to their advantage during the negotiation phase (Moran 1991).

Rituals are a fundamental part of Chinese culture, including business. They serve many different purposes, but their main purpose is to keep encounters formal and controlled, thus allowing everyone to maintain *mianzi.* A common ritual that appears to be controversial in the West is gift-giving.

Gift Giving

Gift giving is a difficult concept for Westerners to understand because they have been taught to trust in laws rather than people. This makes Westerners tend to review the gift-giving practice as a bribe.

In the Chinese perspective, this is not a bribe but *keqi,* a cultural obligation. It is an obligation because *keqi* dictates that, to save *mianzi,* a gift should be given when first meeting someone in a formal setting. It also dictates that a gift be given for utilizing someone's *guanxi* to obtain favors from a friend. *Mianzi* also dictates that those who have money, power, or influence must use it to assist others within their *guanxi* network (De Keijzer 1994). Due to these non-Western rules, Western companies are often choosing to enter into IJVs as their form of investment because that way they can allow their Chinese partners to deal with the cultural aspects. After the deal is made and the joint venture is operating, the Chinese side usually handles all the cultural aspects, while keeping the Western partner in the dark (De Keijzer 1994).

"Chinese are conditioned to express appreciation in tangible ways, such as gifts and other favors. They expect appreciation in a concrete way when they do someone a favor" (De Mente 1989: 89). Giving gifts is an expression of that appreciation; it is a part of Chinese culture and is directly linked to *keqi, mianzi* and *guanxi.* Given its importance in the culture, it is not surprising that there is a ritual involved in giving gifts. It serves to maintain a certain distance and formality, thus keeping it impersonal.

The timing of the gift is also important. The most important one occurs at the first formal meeting at the host party. This allows the foreign company to thank the host for throwing the party in their honor. It is also a sign of respect and gives everyone involved *mianzi*.

In other situations, some of which will not be so formal, the Chinese will decline the gift two or three times before accepting it. They will do this even if they want it and requested the person to bring it to them. The declining of the gift is simply being polite and is part of *keqi*. (De Mente 1989) This is important for foreigners to understand because they need to offer the gift several times to allow the person to accept it. There will be times that *mianzi* will dictate that they really cannot accept a gift, and they will decline the gift, but it is difficult for foreigners to understand the difference. A rule of thumb is to offer the gift three times. After the third time accept their answer.

The gifts don't need to be of a high value, but it is critical that the highest-ranking person in the room gets the best gift. There are gifts that are considered in bad luck due to Chinese beliefs. A couple of these gifts include a fan and a clock. Their pronunciations are similar to the word for "death." There are exceptions to giving clocks, one of which is a watch. The word watch is pronounced differently than the word death, therefore it is not associated with bad luck. The cost of the gift is not as important as the giving of the gift. The purpose of the gift is respecting someone's *mianzi* and following the rules of *keqi* and *renqing*.

An example of the depth of this custom can be found in a story my informant told me about what happened to a Chinese friend who lived and worked in America in 1999. A new American sales manager wanted to congratulate a Chinese salesperson for doing a good job with this difficult product line. The sales manager gave the Chinese salesperson, in a semi-formal way, a little promotional clock. The Chinese salesperson accepted it (she had to accept the gift to save *mianzi*). The idea, however, of receiving a clock as a gift from anyone anywhere was more than she could take. So, while the sales manager was gone, the salesperson actually threw a silver coin into the sales manager's office and then told herself that she had purchased the clock at a discount.

To the Chinese salesperson, the clock was a sign of bad luck. The intent of the gift did not matter. Imagine giving a clock to the head of a Chinese company at a host party for all in attendance to see. This would be a major loss of *mianzi*.

Other taboos surrounding gift giving include wrapping the gift in white wrapping paper. In the past dead bodies were wrapped in a white cloth for burial. Therefore, giving a gift wrapped in white is like presenting death with a bow. Another taboo involves the color red. To the Chinese this is a festive color full of good luck, unless it pertains to a person's name. On the tombs, the person's name is painted in red. Thus, on business cards, the company's name or the person's name or title should never be in red. For business cards the best colors are gold and black on off-white paper. This taboo on red also holds true for names during a presentation.

To the Chinese, friendship and obligation are fundamental keys to establishing business contacts and partners. The process of meeting and establishing the groundwork for a friendship is made even more difficult for many Chinese hindered by the rituals and gifts that surround the process. That process can be stopped or even destroyed by a host's need for revenge if a loss of *mianzi* occurs. These are serious situations to the Chinese and cannot be taken lightly.

Chapter 6

The Negotiation Process

The purpose of this chapter is to provide a step-by-step introduction to the process of conducting international business negotiations to establish business contracts or International Joint Ventures (IJV). Please note that the term "contract" will mean any business contract; that includes the establishment of an IJV.

This chapter divides the negotiation process into three components, pre-negotiation, formal negotiation, and post-negotiation. The purpose of the pre-negotiation section is to acquaint the negotiating team with the tools they will need to successfully negotiate a business contract. The formal negotiation section will discuss the actual negotiation process, including indications of intent. The post-negotiation section discusses the implementation of the contract and the new negotiations that *will* follow.

Pre-negotiation

The goal of the pre-negotiation process is to provide the negotiating team with the tools they need to successfully conduct business negotiations during the formal and post-negotiation process. This preparation involves three systematic steps—team selection, research, and the development of a clear plan.

The first step, team selection, is the most vital because the people that a company selects to represent them in a foreign country will determine the perception that the "other team" has of the company. The company needs to select people with a global cultural perspective who enjoy meeting and associating with people from all backgrounds and walks of life. Their attitude in this area is vital because they will need to work with people who have different ideas about life, business, culture, religion, money, family, as well as a host of other issues. The negotiating team, therefore, needs to be open minded to new ideas and not to have a culturally superior attitude. They need to be able to adjust their negotiating strategies to the culturally accepted norms. The team selection is a critical first step because it will be their job to negotiate the cultural issues that conceal hidden agendas and latent intents.

The second step is to conduct research on the counterpart's cultural perspective, because it reveals their cultural mindset or how they think. The preliminary research should include researching a combination of their religion, philosophy, government, politics, law, economy, and history as well as other areas that may become important. The preliminary research will indicate what specific aspects should be researched in more detail. In this case study of China, the preliminary research indicated that more emphasis needed to be placed on religion, (even though the PRC is an atheist country) as well as on philosophy, history and politics, in order to develop an understanding of the four cultural complexes. Another aspect of this research includes understanding the local economic organization as well as local business strategies and tactics.

Understanding the host country's perspective is important because it gives clues to why they do things a certain way. In the case of the PRC, the Chinese follow the four cultural complexes. It is better for foreigners to leave their egos at home because, when dealing with the Chinese, it is better to be humble, polite, and to establish good *mianzi* and *guanxi*, then to use gunboat strategies and tactics.

The third step is to utilize the information gathered in step two to develop and negotiate a clear plan of how to win a specific contract. The research will already have indicated what the other side's cultural and business priorities, strategies and tactics are. Once the Cultural Translators understand the information gathered in step two, they will need to evaluate their personal and the company's *mianzi* and *guanxi* positions in relation to the specific con-tract, in order to assess whether or not they are in a position to actually be awarded the contract.

If they are not, then they need to forgo a losing battle and commit their resources to earning *mianzi* and developing *guanxi*, because, as the research has indicated, the Chinese have already chosen the company that will be awarded the contract. If the foreign company's *mianzi* and *guanxi* positions are not already strong, the odds of their being awarded the contract are very slim. If, however, they are in a good position, then they will need to formulate a clear plan, which includes increase their lobbying efforts, giving presentations, creating counter strategies and tactics, and utilizing their *guanxi* to promote their bid and to discover any undisclosed issues with the project.

The lobbying needs to be both broad and focused in areas that can directly benefit the foreign company. Most broadly, this would include advertising in professional journals, visiting officials at both the local level and at the national level in Beijing. The focused efforts will include inviting national and local officials to tour the foreign company's headquarters and other facilities. There will also need to be several flawless presentations and several formal and informal dinners. These efforts demonstrate to the Chinese officials that the foreign company is interested in China for the long term and that it is highly reliable with the best technology suited for their priorities; and that the company is financially strong. One major purpose of the lobbying is to make the Chinese officials feel safe in choosing this company for the project.

Presentations play a key role in the lobbying efforts, but they need to be consistent, sharp, and reliable. They need to be reliable and consistent each and every time because the Chinese are looking for contradictions in the presentations that can be used later to obtain a strategic advantage during the negotiation process. Being consistent means every time the presentation is given, that the projectors, televisions, VCRs, and speakers all work. It also means that the contents of the presentations need to be consistent as well. Consistency is important because once the decision is made to proceed with the foreign company's proposal; the Chinese will discuss every presentation that was given, looking for discrepancies to be exploited.

The presentations also need to be sharp and reliable to let the potential Chinese partners know that the company's negotiating team members are competent and capable of conducting the formal negotiation process. The presentations should be focused on convincing the Chinese that the company is serious about doing business in China and that their products are produced using advanced technology and are of the highest quality and are marketed at reasonable prices.

The presentations are a key factor in the pre-negotiation process because the Chinese will ask that the presentation be given many times to various groups and sometimes to the same group twice. Then, without warning, the Chinese team will be replaced and the presentations will need to be given again. One Ericsson negotiator described the process:

> "You have to learn how to make presentations... you have to present your technology and company many times to different groups... and sometimes the same group comes back, but of course, they don't remember anything from the earlier presentation... they ask the same questions... I think they do this to check you" (Ghauri N.d.:11).

The presentation material should also be provided in both English and Chinese.

It is also important to keep in mind that business services in other countries are often not available 24/7 as they are in the US. Therefore, it is recommended that the team take with them computers, printers, and backups to create any promotional material that the Chinese might need or request. It is also important to provide the presentation material to both the end-users and to governmental officials.

Another situation that can occur during the presentation process is a lack of translators because, generally, the foreign company will have a team of 3–4 people and one translator, while the Chinese will bring 10–12 people to the presentation. A single translator can easily become overwhelmed during the informal discussions that occur after the presentation. This is critical because the Chinese conduct much of their business during these informal discussions. Therefore, it is best to hire one translator per team member for the presentations. The Cultural Translator needs to keep in mind that the Chinese are evaluating every step of this process. If the presentation goes well, but the questions after the presentation were not able to be answered or addressed due to a shortage of translators or a lack of time, this will be seen as a problem by the Chinese. It is a problem because it is a sign of a failure to communicate due to the foreign company not being prepared, staffed, and organized. The Chinese will be asking themselves, if the foreign company is having problems communicating at this stage, how well will they communicate if there is a problem?

The Cultural Translators will also need to prepare strategies and tactics to counter the ones that the Chinese will be utilizing during the negotiation process. The best countermeasure is good *mianzi* and *guanxi*, but sometimes that is not enough, because the Chinese negotiators' first loyalties are to their company and fellow team members with whom they have exceptional *mianzi* and *guanxi*. Other strategies and tactics will need to be utilized. The

Cultural Translators, therefore, will need to be well versed in how to use the four cultural complexes and the strategies of Sun-Tzu and the 36 Strategies. This will prepare them to anticipate the strategies and tactics that the Chinese will use during the negotiation process. For example, the Phillips negotiator that was discussed in Chapter five, understood the strategies and tactics that the Chinese use, therefore, he knew how to counter their attempt to obtain a strategic advantage by reacting calmly, not agreeing or disagreeing, and then bringing it up again during an informal meeting with the Chinese official. Another example was the Ericsson negotiations and the use of a Western-style living arrangements for their executive. If they would have understood the four cultural complexes and Sun-Tzu's strategies and the 36 Strategies, then they would have realized during the negotiation process that this was not a matter that would be a deal breaker, but was one that would not be acceptable to the Chinese.

In addition, by understanding the four cultural complexes, the Cultural Translators can use their good *mianzi* and *guanxi* to increase their lobbying efforts, to obtain additional information about the contract, and to show the Chinese that they know how to successfully work with them.

Formal Negotiations

The formal negotiation process is where most companies believe the battle begins and ends; in China however, this is merely the middle of the battle. By the time the formal negotiations start, the

Chinese have already gathered intelligence on the foreign company, including contacting people within their *guanxi* network to find out all they can on the foreign company and their technology. They have had meetings with all their people to discuss investment options and they have already come to a group consensus regarding the final structure of the contract. This will include their position on all points of negotiation, what their bottom line will be, and what they are expecting the foreign company to concede. Everything that they can control or decide will have been predetermined and confirmed by a committee even before the first host party has been planned. They take this approach because, according to Sun-Tzu, every battle is won or lost before the battle has begun. To the Chinese, this is especially true for the negotiation process.

Three major components of the formal negotiation process are formal meetings, informal meetings, and indications of intent.

Formal Meetings

The formal meetings are where the purpose of the contract is discussed and where the points of negotiation are established. These points of negotiation are to be taken seriously and there are several points that the foreign negotiating team needs to address prior to signing a contract to establish an IJV. The most important has to do with the long-term vision or goals of the IJV and of the parent companies: are they compatible and realistic? Once this is agreed upon, the next question is who will control this common vision. In the early 1980s the Chinese would take a minority stake in a company, but as more companies wanted to enter the PRC, and as they became more experienced in working with Western companies, the CA has been insisting on a controlling share of IJVs. Ownership or control is important in China because there is no veto power, meaning that the minority shareholder does not have recourse if they disagree with what the majority partner wants to do. A 50/50 equity split will still be countered by the Chinese holding a majority on the board of directors, therefore there needs to be at least a 51/49 equity split to ensure control.

A few other points of interest would include the management structure, duration of the IJV, dispute settlements procedures, management transition issues, political concerns, and human resources and technology. Negotiating issues of human resources and technology are particularly important.

Human resources are going to be a vital part of any IJV. One of the issues will be how many foreigners will be employed in the IJV in the PRC. Others include training and who will pay for it, as well as how people will be evaluated and promoted.

Another area that needs to be addressed carefully is technology. There are several reasons why this is critical. The first has to do with the lack of a fair and efficient legal framework in China. Another involves the question of who will own the results of the IJVs' research and development technology. According to Chinese law, the right to use and transfer these research and development results belongs to the Chinese. A company, wanting to conduct research and development, therefore, needs to be careful or they might develop additional Chinese competition because the Chinese can transfer that new technology to other Chinese companies or even sell it to competitors.

Informal Meetings

Informal meetings will happen while socializing after the formal meetings, during informal dinners, and during other casual interactions between people from the negotiating teams. This is an important part of the formal negotiation process for three reasons. First, these opportunities are used by the Chinese to see if the foreign company is compatible and open to the Chinese way of conducting business. Second, this is where a good portion of the difficult points of negotiation will be resolved. Third, informal meetings are linked with their strategy of deception to obtain additional information about problems with technology, supply, and consistency, about the foreign company's own organizational issues, and about conflicts within the foreign negotiating team. As this book has pointed out earlier, the Chinese find this type of intelligence gathering both ethical and natural. Their goal in this process is to discover if the foreign company has any hidden agendas or latent intents in order to get the best contract they can negotiate.

The story, reported in chapter five, of the Motorola negotiator is a good example of how an informal dinner can be used by a foreign company's negotiator to achieve a strategic advantage during the negotiation phase. In that example, a Chinese negotiator told the Motorola negotiators that there was a problem with Motorola's technology in Thailand. The Motorola negotiator did not confirm or deny the situation. Once the Motorola negotiator was able to call and discuss the issue with his Thailand counterpart, he found out that there were no technical problems in Thailand. He did not bring this up at the next negotiation session and make an issue of it. Instead he quietly brought it up at a casual dinner with a particular Chinese negotiator and informed him that he had checked on his issue and that there was no problem and he gave him the telephone number of their counterpart in Thailand to confirm, if he wished. This was a *mianzi* saving move by the Motorola negotiator. He was able to inform the Chinese that they both knew that there was not a problem with their technology in Thailand, but he did it without causing the Chinese negotiator to lose *mianzi*. Thus, he was able to turn the situation in to a strategic advantage for Motorola. The next day, the Chinese negotiator was ready to approve the deal.

Be assured that this was a deliberate negotiation strategy that was intended to cause a cultural conflict that the Chinese would be able to use to their strategic advantage by calling it a loss of *mianzi*. It is certain that the Chinese negotiating team had met prior to the next formal negotiating meeting and discussed this incident. The Chinese, as a group, decided to move forward on the deal and this particular negotiator was now their spokesperson. The Chinese will always work from a group consensus, spoken through various voices, but of one mind and committed to their plan.

Indications of Intent

The "indication of intent" is a multi-step process that includes submitting a letter of intent, then a formal proposal, negotiating a contract, and securing the final approval. What makes this seemingly straightforward process challenging when establishing an IJV is culture. In China, this means the four cultural complexes, Chinese negotiating strategies, and the political and governmental structure.

As discussed earlier, the Chinese negotiators' actions are limited to those permitted by the four cultural complexes of *mianzi, keqi, guanxi,* and *renqing.* Cultural Translators must understand this and must be able to determine the difference between the culturally-defined responses of *mianzi* and *keqi* and responses that indicate a true interest in conducting business. This difference is commonly seen when 'yes' means 'maybe', and 'maybe' means 'no'.

When 'YES' means 'MAYBE' and 'MAYBE' means 'NO'

To fully understand this statement requires recognition that saving *mianzi* is the most important thing to a Chinese businessperson, and that cultural dictates also require them to follow *keqi.* This is their cultural mindset; this is how they think. A 'yes', therefore does not mean that they wish to conduct business; it means that they will examine the possibility of pursuing what the foreign company proposes. There is a difference. The difference is that the Chinese businesspersons will first need to check with others within their company to see if their company is even interested in pursuing a business partnership with this foreign company. They answer 'yes' to the initial inquiry because *keqi* dictates that they be polite at all times to protect the foreigner, or any other person—Chinese or otherwise—from any embarrassment or loss of *mianzi.* At the same time, the Chinese businessman needs to save his own *mianzi*, therefore the answer must be a 'yes', because 'no' is not a polite response.

If on the other hand, if the Chinese are not at all interested in the idea of conducting business with this foreign company, for whatever reason, they will answer with a 'maybe', because *keqi* dictates that they be polite and 'no' would not be polite. Therefore, a 'yes' means 'maybe' and 'maybe' means 'no' and would be so understood by other Chinese.

Once the Chinese agree to discuss the possibility of a partnership, the next step of the negotiation process is a letter of intent, which is the first step to the real process of negotiation.

Letter of Intent

When drafting up the "letter of intent", it is important for the negotiation team to keep in mind that, at this stage, the goal is not a "good deal", but a "successful" joint venture. The letter therefore should only outline "the scope of the project, the activities to be conducted, and the financial structure of the new entity" (Engholm 1994: 226). This is not a binding contract and should just be an outline of the project, for it will serve as the basis for the subsequent contract, and the contract may be limited by the specifics of the letter of intent (Engholm 1994).

While the letter of intent is being considered, the parties should also agree to conduct a preliminary feasibility study and to draft a pre-incorporation agreement. These three documents should reveal whether or not the two companies have compatible long-term goals.

The preliminary feasibility study should determine whether or not the two organizations are compatible. This is important for the success of the IJV because an IJV brings together two culturally structured organizations to form a third corporation that must be able to work within both parent organizational cultures. It is critical that the organizations be compatible because differences in cultural assumptions, especially ethnocentric ones, will reinforce stereotypes and social boundaries between groups. The result will be the emergence of a culturally fragmented IJV (DiBella 1994: 319). Cultural incompatibility negatively influences the decision-making process and the implementation of decisions, due to the differences in cultural backgrounds of managers and workers within the IJV. Thus it is important that the negotiators explore the long-term effects of their venture to ensure that its goals are compatible with the parent companies' long-term structure, and short- and long-term goals (DiBella 1994).

To ensure that a long-range view is maintained during the negotiation process, pre-incorporation agreements should be drawn up at this time as well, because they can decrease the number of future problems by increasing the transparency of the two companies and by exposing some hidden agendas. This agreement should spell out the board structure, financial arrangements, arbitration procedures, conflict resolution procedures, policies toward the host county, and the duration of the venture itself. (Zeira 1995). One aspect that should be explicitly addressed in the conflict resolution domain is theft. Most of these IJV will be dealing with expensive equipment and/or spare parts which, on occasion, will go missing or be shown as never having been delivered.

This is the case with one of my informants. They had a $100,000 part disappear. The Chinese response was that they did not know where it was and that they could not move forward until they had it. The American partner was a small company that really did not want to take a $100,000 loss on a part that was stolen while under the care of their Chinese partner. But they had no choice; it was either send another part or close the venture, because their Chinese partner refused to move on the issue, stating that they could not afford to replace the part. The American partner sent anther part and my informant's task was to ensure that the part was delivered.

As the negotiators are focusing on these issues, the Cultural Translator needs to be focused on strategy because the Chinese will be looking for opportunities to quietly apply various strategies from Sun Tzu and the 36 Strategies to the negotiation process. These applied strategies will be difficult to recognize because they will be presented as problems with the technology, cultural issues, time delays, as well as a host of other issues, but goal will be clear: to deceive the foreign company into giving up too much.

The Proposal

Before the Chinese partner submits the proposal to the CA for their approval, the preliminary feasibility study should be completed to ensure that the organizations involved have compatible goals. In addition, the pre-incorporation paper outlining the various aspects of the organization should be agreed upon. All the participating partners must sign the letter of intent. The Chinese partner then submits the proposal to all the relevant Chinese authorities, complete with the preliminary feasibility study (Engholm 1994).

If everyone accepts the proposal, then the CA will request a full feasibility study. In the past the CA did not care about this type of study, then they realized that failed ventures cost them money, time, technology, and other valuable commodities. Therefore, a full feasibility study needs to be conducted by an objective third party (Engholm 1994).

The Contract

Once the full feasibility study is completed and approved by all the agencies that need to approve it, a contract can be drafted and signed. The CA is layered in its bureaucracy and needs to be kept informed of any changes to the contract. It is the Chinese partner's responsibility to keep the proper authorities informed at all times of any changes. It is also essential for the foreign company to request copies of all the forms submitted for their records.

The full feasibility study and the contract are submitted to the relevant authorities for official approval. The biggest risk at this point is to have the CA override local authority and rescind agreements on investment incentives or even withdraw the entire authorization for the project due to larger national interests. This can also be a negotiating strategy. If a project has had some problems and the Chinese want out because of a loss of *mianzi* that occurred earlier, or if they were just using the foreign company to get a better price from another company, this is where the foreign company will find out. This gives the Chinese a way out of the agreement without the loss of *mianzi*. It also gives them a chance to reopen negotiations at the last minute, thus putting pressure on the foreign negotiating team to give more than they wanted to, just to put the contract together and to get home (Engholm 1994).

Another aspect of the contract that is difficult for foreign companies to understand is that the Chinese will first establish general principles, and then worry about details later. As Sun-Tzu points out, conditions change and that will affect the details. The principles, however, will remain constant. Thus, they will not sign a long-term detailed contract. The contract needs to be simplified, because to the Chinese a contract is a commercial agreement, not a legal document, and is not the last word on anything. The Chinese will insist that their agreements and responsibilities be spelled out. They will not, however, insist that the foreign company's agreements and responsibilities be spelled out in the contract. This allows the Chinese to let the court decide if the Chinese were at fault if there is a disagreement. The Chinese will take a legalistic view of the contracts and will not feel bound by anything that is not explicitly stated in the contract (De Mente 1989).

The Approval Process

Once the contract is approved by all the agencies, then the companies must register the new corporation with the Ministry of Foreign Trade and Economic Cooperation (MOFTEC). The foreign company may need to prod the Chinese company to ensure that it is fulfilling all the requirements. A local authority may have approved the venture, but that does not mean they have completed all the requirements to make it legal.

The final approval process is just as complicated as the preliminary process has been thus far. There are two types of decisions that the CA makes in approving an IJV in China. They first examine the technical aspects and then the administrative structure. The technical aspects involve everything from the logistical issues of the choice of technology, to the training of the workers, to where the actual building will be built. The administrative decision covers everything from the structure of the board of directors, to the amount of hard currency the Chi-nese company is to contribute, to who has the controlling interest. In both areas, the venture is examined from many angles, and then changes might be sent back to the local authority for their approval as well.

The foreign negotiating team needs to keep in mind that they are not just negotiating with another company, as it may appear. They are either negotiating with members of the local authority or the CA, and in some instances, both. This is significant because the local and central authorities' priorities are different. The local authority is focused on their particular area and what it needs, while the CA's priorities are focused on the bigger national interest, which will vary depending on the region and time.

Post-Negotiation Negotiations

In China, post-negotiation negotiations almost always occur because of their view of contracts. The

Chinese view the contract as a business agreement, not as a legal document; therefore, as the business environment changes, so can the obligations of the contract. This is not to say that the Chinese don't honor their contracts or obligations, because they do, but there are cases where they didn't honor various types of obligations for various reasons. A case in point is what happened to managing director at Ericsson when the Chinese side refused to place him in a Western-standard of housing, as outlined in the contract (Ghauri N.d.).

The previous example and the information contained in this section regarding the post-negotiation negotiations came from a paper written by Pervez N. Ghauri and Tony Fang. Pervez Ghauri is a Professor of Marketing at the University of Groningen in the Netherlands and Tony Fang is with the International Graduate School of Management and Industrial Engineering at Linkoping University in Sweden. Part of their paper, *The Chinese Business Negotiation Process: A Socio-cultural Analysis*, discusses the issue of post-negotiations in China and is the main source of information for this section unless otherwise noted.

Ghauri and Fang's research found that foreign companies should keep what they called the five P's in mind during the post-negotiation phase—priority, patience, price, precision, and people.

Priority

As the PRC swung open its huge rusted iron doors to economic reforms in 1978, Western companies rushed in to exploit an old Western business saying; "the first one to market wins." As most of these companies discovered, the PRC was not the West and this saying does not apply. What did apply then, and still does today, are the four cultural complexes and Chinese priorities. In the case of the PRC, the CA is in charge of everything, and all of the SOEs follow all the priorities, policies and plans established by the CA. As this book and Ghauri and Fang's research have indicated, companies who want large state contracts need to understand and be sensitive to the CA's social and economic policies, even if they don't agree with them. They also need to stay focused on the priorities of the CA because these are indicators where the CA is interested in investing. As indicated in the economics section, the debt ridden TVEs are going to be high on their priority list for some time, as are energy, transportation and telecommunications. One way that foreign firms can keep up with the changing priorities of the CA is to develop friendships with officials at the local and national level, and to invite Chinese partners to the home country for a visit. It is called taking the tiger out of the jungle; by removing your Chinese partners from the PRC, it allows them to relax and talk more freely.

Patience

Patience is a virtue that is needed to do business in the PRC. Due to the vast areas where everything from the infrastructure to basic living conditions is underdeveloped, problems will occur. In addition, there are numerous organizations and departments involved in any negotiation process, and they all need to come to a common consensus before making a decision. Therefore, time is needed to allow them to meet and decide on a plan of action.

Another aspect that consumes time is creating *mianzi* and developing *guanxi* with all of the people within these organizations and departments. Time must be invested because the Chinese are exposed to political pressures that can create problems when there is a lack of mutual trust between the Chinese and foreign negotiating teams. This is why foreign companies wanting to conduct business in the PRC need to look at the long term, be patient, and never show emotion.

Price

Price can be a difficult negotiation point because the Chinese believe in establishing a trusting relationship with their partners. Therefore, if the foreign company reduces their price too much, the Chinese negotiators will think that there is a hidden agenda or motive. The result will be that the foreign company will lose *mianzi* to their Chinese partner. On the other hand, if the foreign company did not build in a negotiating buffer on their price, and rejects all requests by the Chinese for a price reduction, they will view this as an insult and a loss of *mianzi*. It is an insult because they are not following *keqi* or doing them a favor. In addition, the Chinese must inform their supervisors that they were not able to negotiate a reduction in price. The result will be an act of revenge either at the next round, or later when the timing is better for them. The idea of revenge needs to stay in the Cultural Translators mind at all times because *renqing* means reciprocal, but it does not mean that it can only be positive. It can also be a negative reciprocal gesture.

The foreign company needs to build in a price buffer and slowly allow the Chinese to negotiate them down to that level. As explained earlier, the foreign company must have a detailed plan of exactly what they are willing to give before they leave home for the PRC. Then they can allow the Chinese negotiating team to negotiate the price down to that level. This saves both groups' *mianzi*. This is the same process the Chinese are using against the foreign company.

Another issue is the cost of foreign personnel in the PRC, a problem that Ericsson became aware of to late. The solution is quite simple; when doing business with a third-world country, don't expect them to pay for an expatriate to live in conditions equal to those in the first world. In some cases it will happen, but the host country will not be happy about the situation. If the foreign company is expecting these types of arrangements they must prepared to pay for them. A solution to the problem is to not send people with big luxury-demanding egos, but Cultural Translators who understand that the living conditions are going to be different.

Precision

As discussed earlier, the Chinese will want to see presentations over and over again to ensure that everything is accurate. If there is a mistake in the presentation, the foreign company will lose credibility and it will be exploited during the negotiation process. It is also important to give them as much accurate and precise information regarding the product as possible, because they will be using this information for comparison in examining other offers. Therefore the foreign firm needs to provide the Chinese with as much detailed and precise specification as possible to facilitate the Chinese decision-making process.

People

As discussed in the cultural and legal sections, the Chinese believe and trust in people, not contracts. Therefore a people-orientated approach needs to be taken in China. Cultural Translators need to take the time to develop *mianzi*. This will place them in a better position to negotiate with the Chinese than a negotiator who just wants to negotiate the contract and go home. This is important, because people are extended *guanxi*, not companies, and it is the personal connections that make things happen in China. A personal relationship is one that is not just based on business; the foreign negotiators need to know how many children their Chinese counterpart has. They must be concerned with their interest and must discuss other topics than just work-related ones. A foreigner needs to remember that in China, people come first.

Chapter 7

Making the Point

According to Buddhism, odd numbers are lucky, therefore, the purpose of chapter seven is to ensure that the paper ends on a lucky chapter.

Bibliography

Adler, Nancy
    1991 International Dimensions of Organizational Behavior, Second Edition. The Kent International Dimensions of Business Series. Boston: PWS-KENT Publishing Company.

AFP, AP
    1997 China reform is long-term and gradual, officials say. International Herald Tribune, September 15:2

AFP, Reuter
    1996 18 to be charged in Beijing for $3 billion corruption scandal. Electronic document, http://www.asia1.comsg/straitstimes/pages/ stone4.html, accessed, April 3.

    1996 Chinese leaders discuss ways to make SEZs more effective. Singapore Press Holdings Ltd, April 4.

Agence France-Presse
    1997 Chinese near vote on central committee. International Herald Tribune, September 18: 4.

    1997 China's Party leaders nod and wink at Marx. International Herald Tribune, September 19: 4.

Alter, Jonathan
    1998 On the Road in China. In The New China. Theme issue. Newsweek, June 29:30.

Associated Press
    1997 China's tax collectors on a roll at McDonald's. International Harald Tribune, September 11:17.

Bibliography

Barnouw, Victor
    1985 Culture and Personality. Belmont: Wadsworth Publishing Company.

Binder, Michaela, Lefort, Maineult, Meng, and Yun
    1998 Negotiating joint ventures in China: Recommendations for foreign companies. Electronic document http://www.admin.uottawa.ca/ staff/schaan/Groupe4.html, accessed on May 30, 2000.

Bonavia, David
    1989 The Chinese: Revised Edition. London: Penguin Books.

Briody, Elizabeth K.
    1995 On Trade and Cultures. Trade and Culture. March-April:5–6.

Burstein, Daniel and Arne DeKeijzer
    1998 Big Dragon China's Future: What it means for business, the economy, and the global order. New York: Simon and Schuster.

C. K.
    1997 More steps to take in long march to WTO. Electronic document, http://www.iht.com/iht/sup/081297/chi-1.html, accessed, November 28.

Chen, Chunlai
    1997a The composition and location determinants of foreign direct investment in China's manufacturing. Unpublished MS, Chinese Economies Research Center, the University of Adelaide.

    1997b The Evolution and main features of Chinas foreign direct investment policies. Unpublished MS, Chinese Economies Research Center, the University of Adelaide.

    1997c Provincial characteristics and foreign direct investment location decision within China. Unpublished MS,

Chinese Economies Research Center, the University of Adelaide.

Chi, Ning
1999 Township firms urged to innovate. China Daily, June 25:2.

Chian, Thian Shian, Philip Lam, Lim Soon Tong, and Zhang Xiliang
1996 Town and Village Enterprises in Jiangsu. In Business Opportunities in the Yangtze River Delta, China. Nanyang Business Report Series. Tan Teck Meng, Low Aik Meng, John J. Williams, Cao Yong, and Shi Yuwei, eds. Pp. 229–258. Singapore.

China Daily
1999 'Silicon Valley' takes shape: Zhongguancun to focus on the development of high-tech sector. China Daily, June 22: 3.

1999 Corrupt officials punished. China Daily, June 14: 2.

1999 Vice-mayor punished for receiving bribes. China Daily, June 14: 3.

1997 Jiang Zemin: General Secretary of the CPC Central Committee. Electronic document, http://www.chinadaily.net/cndy/ history/15/jprofile.html, accessed, November 27.

1997 Li Peng: Standing Committee Member of CPC Politburo. Electronic document, http://www.chinadaily.net/cndy/ history/15/lprofile.html, accessed, November 27.

1997 Zhu Rongji: Standing Committee Member of CPC Politburo. Electronic document, http://www.chinadaily.net/cndy/ history/15/zprofile.html, accessed, November 27.

Bibliography

1997 Li Ruihuan: Standing Committee Member of CPC Politburo. Electronic document, http://www.chinadaily.net/cndy/ history/15/hprofile.html, accessed, November 27.

1997 Hu JinTao: Standing Committee Member of CPC Politburo. Electronic document, http://www.chinadaily.net/cndy/ history/15/tprofile.html, accessed, November 27.

1997 Wei Jianxing: Standing Committee Member of CPC Politburo. Electronic document, http://www.chinadaily.net/cndy/ history/15/wprofile.html, accessed, November 27.

1997 Li Lanqing: Standing Committee Member of CPC Politburo. Electronic document, http://www.chinadaily.net/cndy/ history/15/qprofile.html, accessed, November 27.

1997 Employment issue not to cause social unrest: labor minister. www.chinadaily.net November 27.

1997 Ownership form and democracy should accord with national conditions, says theorist. www.chinadaily.net, November 27.

Chinoy, Mike
1997 China Live: Two decades in the heart of the dragon. Atlanta: Turner Publishing, Inc.

Christiansen, Flemming and Shirin Rai
1996 Chinese Politics and Society: An Introduction. New York: Prentice Hall.

Chu, Chin-Ning
1991 The Asian Mind Game. New York: Rawson Associates.

Crowell, Todd and David Hsieh

1997 Now, the Jian Zemin Era. AsiaWeek, September 26, Electronic document, http://www.asiaweek/current/issue/cs2.html, accessed, September 26.

Dale, Reginald
1997 Which future for China: threat or positive force? International Herald Tribune, September 19: 13.

De Keijzer, Arne J.
1992 China Business Strategies for the '90s. Berkeley, Pacific View Press.

De Mente, Boye
1989 Chinese Etiquette & Ethic in Business: A penetrating analysis of the morals and values that shape the Chinese business personality. Lincolnwood, IL, NTC Business Books.

1996 Chinese Etiquette & Ethic in Business: A penetrating analysis of the morals and values that shape the Chinese business personality, second ed. Lincolnwood, IL, NTC Business Books.

Deng, Feng, Norman Solihin, and Ol Tian Poon
1996 The Choice of Relevant Investment Forms in China: Wholly Foreign-owned Versus Joint Venture Enterprises. *In* Business Opportunities in Sichuan Province, China. Nanyang Business Report Series. Tan Teck Meng, Low Aik Meng, Chew Soon Beng, John J. Williams, Cao Yong, and Chen Kang, eds. Pp. 115–124. Singapore.

Dernberger, Robert, Kenneth DeWoskin, Steven Goldstein, Rhoads Murphey, Martin Whyte
1991 The Chinese: Adapting the Past Facing the Future. Ann Arbor: The University of Michigan Center for Chinese Studies Publications.

Dreyer, June Teufel
1996 China's Political System: Modernization and Tradition. Second edition. Boston, Allyn and Bacon.

Bibliography

Dunning, John
    1997 Commentary: How should national governments respond to globalization? The International Executive 39(1): 55–66.

Dutton, Gail.
    1999 Building a Global Brain. Management Review 88(5):34–38.

Economist, the
    1998 The Song of Jiang Zemin. August 8, 35-36.

    1998 China's political cage. August 8, 16.

Economy, Elizabeth
    N.d. The Case Study of China. Electronic document, http://www.utlink.utoronto.ca/www/pcs/state/china/chinasum/htm,accessed on May 30, 2000.

Elliott, Dorina
    1998 Trying to stand on two feet. *In* The New China. Theme issue. Newsweek, June 29:48–49.

Elliott, Michael with George Wehrfritz, Melinda Liu, Dorina Elliott, Karen Breslau, Michael Hirsh, and Mark Hosenball

    1998 Beyond history's Shadow. Newsweek *In* The New China. Theme issue. Newsweek, June 29:20–25.

Engardio, Pete with Jonathan Moore, Christine Hill, and bureau reports
    1996 Time for a reality check in Asia: As the miracle economies slow down, their hidden problems start to appear. BusinessWeek, December 2: 58–66.

Engholm, Christopher
    1994 Doing Business in Asia's Booming "China Triangle": People's Republic of China, Taiwan, and Hong Kong. The Prentice Hall Emerging World Market Series. Englewood Cliffs, NJ, Prentice Hall.

Erickson, Jim, Anne Naham

1997 Playing to the gallery: Chinese are learning the importance of image. AsiaWeek, September 26, electronic document, http://www.asiaweek/current/issue/cs7.html, accessed on September 26.

Faison, Seth.
1997 A gimps of the other side of China's elite. International Herald Tribune, September 1: 2.

Fatehi, Kamal and Deema deSilva
1996 International Communication and Negotiation. *In* International Management: A Cross-Cultural and Functional Perspective. Kamal Fathehi, ed. Pp. 185–226. Upper Saddle River: Prentice Hall.

Ferraro, Gary P.
1994 The Cultural Dimensions of International Business, Second Edition. Englewood Cliffs, NJ, Prentice-Hall, Inc.

Fisher, Glen
1980 International Negotiation: A Cross-Cultural Perspective. New York: Intercultural Press, Inc.

Freeman, Chas W., Jr.
1996 Sino-American Relations: Back to Basics. Foreign Policy (104) Fall:3–17.

Gage, Jonathan and Velisarios Kattoulas.
1997 China lays claim as tigers' successor. International Herald Tribune, September 11:13.

Gao, Wei
1999 Economic ties with L. America to be promoted. China Daily, June 22:5.

Gargan, Edward A.
1990 China's Fate: A people's turbulent struggle with reform and repression 1980–1990. New York: Doubleday.

Ghauri, Pervez N.

N.d. The Chinese Business Negotiation Process: A Socio-Cultural Analysis. . Unpublished MS, Chinese Economies Research Center, the University of Adelaide.

Haley, George, Chin Tiong Tan, Usha Haley
1998 New Asian Emperors: The Overseas Chinese, their Strategies and Competitive Advantages. Oxford: Butterworth Heinemann.

Hirsh, Michael.
1998 Tricks of Trade. *In* The New China. Theme issue. Newsweek, June 29: 40-42.

Hofstede, Geert
1991a Cultures and organizations: software of the mind, Intercultural cooperation and its importance for survival. New York: McGraw-Hill.

1984b Culture's Consequences: International Differences in Work-Related Values. Cross-Cultural Research and Methodology Series, 5. Newbury Park: Sage Publications, Inc.

Irvine, Steven
    1997 Winning the China game. Euromoney (341) September: 64–73.

Jacob, Rahul
    1995 China: a growth beast's rough ride. Electronic document, http://www.fortune.com/pacrimspecial/ specials/asiaspecial/asia.china.html.

Jiang, Zemin
    1997 Jiang Zemin's report to the 15th Party Congress. Electronic document, http://www.chinadaily.net/ cndy/history/15/fulltext.html, accessed, November 25.

Joffe, Ellis
        1975 Between Two Plenums: China's Intraleadership
        Conflict, 1959–1962. Michigan Papers in Chinese Studies, 22. Ann Arbor: The University of Michigan Center
        for Chinese Studies.

Kissinger, Henry A.
    1998 No Room for Nostalgia. *In* The New China. Theme issue. Newsweek, June 29:50–52.

Klitgard, Thomas and Karen Schiele
    1997 The Growing U.S. Trade Imbalance with China. Current Issues in Economics and Finance, Feberal Reserve Bank of New York 3(7).

Kotkin, Joel
    1992 Tribes: How Race, Religion and Identity Determine Success in the New Global Economy. New York: Random House, Inc.

Kristof, Nicholas and Sheryl Wudunn
    1995 China Wakes: The struggle for the soul of a rising power. New York: Vintage Books.

Kroeniger, Petra, Catherine Pottier, Richard Zhang, and Gunter Sammer

Bibliography

1998 A successful joint venture in Beijing, China. Electronic document, http://www.admin.uottawa.ca/staff/schaan/Groupe3.html, accessed on May 30, 2000.

Kuffel, Christopher
1997 A trading 'Greater China": The economies of China, Hong Kong and Taiwan continue to grow closer. Electronic document, http://www.iht.com/iht/sup/ 081297/chi-2.html, accessed, November 28.

Kwong, Peter
1996 The Chinese Diaspora. Worldbusines: the global perspective, May/June: 26-31.

Kyodo, AFP
1996 Teng-hui rebuffs China's attack on democracy. Electronic document, http://www.asia1.com.sg/straitstimes/pages/stea4.html, accessed, February 1.

Lardy, Nicholas
1992 Foreign trade and economic reform in China, 1978–1990. Cambridge: Cambridge University Press.

Lau, Lawrence
1997 China Unscathed: For Beijing, the currency crisis can be an opportunity. Electronic document, http://www.asiaweek.com/97/1226/feat4.html, accessed, January 5, 1998.

Lee Suay Wah
1996 Feasibility Study on Investment in China. Business Opportunities in Sichuan Province, China. Nanyang Business Report Series. Tan Teck Meng, Low Aik Meng, Chew Soon Beng, John J. Williams, Cao Yong, and Chen Kang, eds. Pp. 115–124. Singapore.

Leland, john and Anna Esaki-Smith
1998 The Rebirth of Cool. *In* The New China. Theme issue. Newsweek, June 29:45–48.

Liu, Melinda

1998 A Fading Scar. *In* The New China. Theme issue. Newsweek, June 29:33–35.

Liu, Weiling
    1999 Loan agreement clinched. China Daily, July 2: 5

Lock, M. F.
    1999 Hong Kong to sell stocks as unit trusts. China Daily, June 22:5.

Macarthney, Jane.
    1995 Risks high in China business. Reuter, transmitted 95-03-17 at 19:39:01 EST.

Malhotra, Angelina and Joe Studwell.
    1995 Revolution's Children. Electronic document, http://www.asia-inc.com/archive/taizi.html, accessed January 3, 1996.

Mastel, Greg
    1996 Beijing at Bay. Foreign Policy (104) Fall:27–34.

Mathur, Ike and Chen Jai-Sheng
    1987 Strategies for Joint Ventures in the People's Republic of China. New York: Praeger Publishing.

Meng Yan.
    1992 China encouraging people to expose crimes. China Daily, June 22:2.

Miller, Myron
    1994 Reflections on current research in International Business. Journal of International Marketing 2(4), Electronic document, http://ciber.bus.msu.edu/jim/abstract/abs-v2n4.htm, accessed on May 30, 2000.

Miller, Robert R., Jack Glen, Frederick Japersen, Yannis Karmokolias
    1999 International Joint Ventures in Developing Countries: Happy Marriages? Statistics for 1970–95. International Finance Corporation, Electronic document.

Bibliography

http://www.ifc.org/economics/pubs/dp29/dp29.htm, accessed May 30, 2000.

Moran, Robert T. and William G. Stripp
    1991 Dynamics of Successful International Business Negotiations. Houston: Gulf Publishing Company.

Mufson, Steven.
    1997a China's New Motto: Survival of the Fittest. International Herald Tribune, September 16:18.

    1997b Chinese get the word on reform: Jiang stresses party control as economy goes private. International Herald Tribune, September 13–14:1,7.

    1997c In China, plea on crackdown: Ex-Leader urges party to reassess assault on students. International Herald Tribune, September 16: 1, 8.

    1997d Handing reins of the Military to 2 Allies, Jiang tightens grasp. International Herald Tribune, September 29: 4.

    1997e China shake-up strengthens Jiang: Removal of No.3 official seen as setback for reformers. International Herald Tribune, September 19: 1, 6.

Naisbitt, John
    1997 Megatrends Asia: Eight Asian Megatrends that are reshaping our world. New York: Touchstone.

Ning, Chen, Marie-Paule Laurent, Polly sun, Satu Teerikangas, Teddy Roche

    1998 How to successfully integrate cultures in Sino-foreign joint-ventures. Electronic document, http://www.admin.uottawa.ca/staff/ schaan/Groupe3.htm, accessed on May 30, 2000.

Ogden, Suzanne

1995 China, sixth edition: People's Republic of China, Taiwan, and Hong Kong. Guilford: Dushkin Publishing Group/Brown and Benchmark Publishers.

Ong, Chong Hien, Ow Kong Chung and Chang Jin Ping
1996 The Choice of Appropriate Partners in China: State-owned enterprises, Companies, or Private Entities. *In* Business Opportunities in Sichuan Province, China. Nanyang Business Report Series. Tan Teck Meng, Low Aik Meng, Chew Soon Beng, John J. Williams, Cao Yong, and Chen Kang, eds. Pp. 125–136. Singapore.

Overholt, William
1996 China after Deng. Foreign Affairs (75)3:63–78.

Parker, Stephen, Gavin Tritt, and Wing Thye Woo
1997 Some Lessons Learned for the Comparison of Transitions in Asia and Eastern Europe. *In* Economies in Transition: Comparing Asia and Europe. Wign Thye Woo, Stephen Parker and Jeffrey Sachs, eds. Pp. 3–18. Cambridge: The MIT Press.

Pfaff, William
1997 Obstacles to China's Development are too often neglected. International Herald Tribune, September 18: 8.

Phatak, Arvind V.
1989 International Dimensions of Management, Second Edition. Boston: PWS-KENT Publishing Company.

Rashid, Ahmed
1997 Go east, go west. Electronic document, http://www.feer.com/ restricted/97 aug_14/energy.html, accessed, August 18.

Reuters
2000 China executes top parliament official for graft. Electronic document, http//www.cnn.com/2000/asianow/east/09/14/crime.china.cheng. reut/index.html, accessed September 14.

Richardson, Michael
    1997 China's military plan: Bid to modernize fast. International Herald Tribune, September 15: 1, 10.

Rohwer, Jim
    1995 Asia Rising: Why America will prosper as Asia's economies boom. New York: Touchstone.

Rosenbaum, Andrew
    1999 Testing Cultural Waters. Management Review 88(7):41–43.

Rosenthal, Elisabeth
    1999 Silence shrouds China. The Wichita Eagle, June 4: 1A, 10A

Ross, Robert
    1996 Enter the Dragon. Foreign Policy (104) Fall:18–26.

Sachs, Jeffrey
    1997 An Overview of Stabilization Issues Facing Economies in Transition. *In* Economies in Transition: Comparing Asia and Europe. Wign Thye Woo, Stephen Parker and Jeffrey Sachs, eds. Pp. 243–256. Cambridge: The MIT Press.

Sawyer, Ralph
    1994 The Art of War. Ralph D. Sawyer, trans. New York: Barnes and Noble.

Schell, Orville
    1994 Mandate of Heaven: A new generation of entrepreneurs, dissidents, bohemians, and technocrats lays claim to China's future. New York: Simon and Schuster.

Seagrave, Sterling
    1995 Lords of the Rim: The Invisible Empire of the Overseas Chinese. New York: G. P. Putnam's Sons.

Segal, Gerald
    The Fate of Hong Kong: The coming of 1997 and what lies beyond. New York: st. Martin's Press.

Shaw, Yu-ming
    1991a Festivals: Traditional Chinese Festivals. Traditional Chinese Culture in Taiwan, 22. Kwang Hwa Publishing Company, Taipei, Taiwan.

    1991b Philosophy: Chinese Philosophical Thought. Traditional Chinese Culture in Taiwan, 21. Kwang Hwa Publishing Company, Taipei, Taiwan.

Shanor, Donald and Constance Shanor
    China Today: How population control, human rights, government repression, Hong Kong, and democratic reform affect life in China...and will shape world events into the new century. New York: St. Martin's Press.

Solt, Michael E .
    1995 Perceptions about Managerial Advancement in the People's Republic of China. The International Executive 37(4): 374, 415–435.

Bibliography

Sprague, Jonathan and Law Siu-Lan
    1997 No currency woes here: But China must tackle SOE and banking reforms. Electronic document, http://www.asiaweek.com/current/ issue/buz3.html, accessed, December 16.

Stuttard, John
    2000 The New Silk Road: Secrets of Business Success in China Today. New York: John Wiley and Sons, Inc.

Sun Jingxuan
    1989 A Spectre Prowls Our Land. *In* Seeds of Fire: Chinese voices of conscience. Geremie Barmé and John Minford, eds. Pp. 121–128. New York The Noonday Press.

Tai, Dian
    1999 Li: Criminal Law should be better applied. China Daily, June 22: 1

Tan, Chin Meng, Chong Chin hui and Tan Kok Fei

    1996 Shanghai's Economic and Trade Zones. *In* Business Opportunities in the Yangtze River Delta, China. Nanyang Business Report Series. Tan Teck Meng, Low Aik Meng, John J. Williams, Cao Yong, and Shi Yuwei, eds. Pp. 229–258. Singapore. Wong Wei, Lee See Tin, Thoo Kah Fah and Tandg Y.Q.

Tang, Min
    1999 High-tech zone to be set up. China Daily, June 15: 3.

Tanzi, Vito
    1998 Corruption Around the World. IMF Staff Papers 45(4): 559–594.

Tarn, Tan and Kao Chen.
    1996 Li Ping outlines economic plan for next five years. Electronic document, http://www.asia1.com/straitstimes/page/stea3.html, accessed on March 5.

Trompenaars, Fons and Charles Hampden-Turner
    1998 Riding the Waves of Culture: Understanding cultural diversity in global business. New York: McGraw-Hill.

Tung, R. L.
    1986 Corporate Executives and Their Families in China: The Need for Cross-Cultural Understanding and Business. Columbia Journal of World Business 21(1):21–25.

Tung, R. L., E. L. Miller
    1990 Managing in the twenty-first Century: The Need for Global Orientation. Management international Review 30(1):5–18.

United States Government
    1999 China 1999 Investment Climate. Electronic document, http://www.usembassy-china.org.cn/english/economics/99101b.html, accessed on May 30, 2000.

    1999 China 1999 Investment Climate, Part 2. Electronic document, http://www.usembassy-china.org.cn/english/economics/991014b.html, accessed on May 30, 2000.

Wang, Yong
    1999 WTO entry promises wider access. China Daily, June 14: 1.

Bibliography
Wang, Zhong-Ming, and Takao Satow
        1994 Leadership Styles and Organizational Effective-
ness in Chinese-Japanese Joint Ventures. Journal of Managerial Psychology 9(4):31–36.

Wartick, Steven and Donna Wood
        1998 International Business and Society. Malden:
Blackwell Publishers, Inc.

Washington Post, The
        1997 Change in China. International Herald Tribune,
September 22:8

Wehrfritz, George
        1998 Maoism at High Speed. *In* The New China.
Theme issue. Newsweek, June 29:47.

Weidenbrum, Murray and Samuel Hughes
        1996 The Bamboo Network: How expatriate Chinese
Entrepreneurs are Creating a New Economic Superpower in
Asia. New York: The Free Press.

Wiseman, Paul
        1999 U. S., global competition to set change into mo-
tion. USA Today, November 18: 1B, 2B.

Weymouth, Lally and Melinda Liu with George Wehrfritz,
Mark Hosenball, and Daniel Klaidman

        1998 A new mystery man. *In* The New China. Theme
issue. Newsweek, June 29:35.

Woo, Wing Thye
        1997 Improving the Performance of Enterprises in
Transition Economies. *In* Economies in Transition: Comparing
Asia and Europe. Wign Thye Woo, Stephen Parker and Jeffrey
Sachs, eds. Pp. 19–40. Cambridge: The MIT Press.

Woodruff, John
        1990 China in search of its future: Reform vs. Repres-
sion, 1982–1989. New York: A Lyle Stuart Book.

Xinhua

1997 Chinese villages now implementing democracy reforms. Electronic document, http://www.chinadaily.net/cndy/history/d1-497.k26.html, accessed, November 26.

1997 Diverse forms of public ownership to promote economic growth, Li Peng. Electronic document, http://www.chinadaily.net/cndy/ history/15/lipent.html, accessed, November 27.

1997 Li Ruihuan emphasizes need to study theory on primary stage of socialism. Electronic document, http://www.chinadaily.net/cndy/ history/15/lrh.html, accessed, November 27.

1997 Liu Huaqing on Party's absolute leadership over army. Electronic document, http://www.chinadaily.net/cndy/history/15/liu.html, accessed, November 27.

1997 Hu Jintao calls for arming Party with Deng Xiaoping Theory. Electronic document, http://www.chinadaily.net/cndy/history/15/hi.html, accessed, November 27.

1997 PLA to hold high banner of Deng Xiaoping Theory. Electronic document, http://www.chinadaily.net/cndy/history/15/pla.html, accessed, November 27.

Bibliography

1997 Employment issue not to cause social unrest: Labor Minister. Electronic document, http://www.chinadaily.net/cndy/history/15/ labor.html, accessed, November 27.

1997 Ownership form and democracy should accord with national conditions, say theorist. Electronic document, http://www.chinadaily.net/ cndy/history/15/own.html, accessed, November 27.

1997 Pary congress to guide China's foreign affairs. Electronic document, http://www.chinadaily.net/cndy/history/15/engtga44.html, accessed, November 27.

1997 Chinese president confidant of success of reform. Electronic document, http://www.chinadaily.net/cndy/history/visit/jconfi.html, accessed, November 27.

1997 China-US joint statement. Electronic document, http://www.chinadaily.net/cndy/history/visit/j-state.html, accessed, November 27.

1999 State backs smaller enterprises. China Daily, June 22:2.

1999 Small loans help farmer families escape poverty. China Daily, June 22: 3.

1999 Sino-US consulting JV to be established. China Daily, June 22:5.

1999 Party role stressed in development. China Daily, July 1: 1.

1999 WTO must heed other countries. China Daily, July 1: 1.

1999 Defense industry crucial: Zhu stresses science's role. China Daily, July 2: 1

Yatsko, Pamela
      1997 Better Mousetraps. Electronic document,
http://www.feer.com/ restricted/97sept_4/tech.html, accessed,
September 5.

Yuan Zhen Cao, Gang Fan and Wing Thye Woo
      1997 Chinese Economic Reforms: pas Successes and Future Challenges. *In* Economies in Transition: Comparing Asia and Europe. Wign Thye Woo, Stephen Parker and Jeffrey Sachs, eds. Pp. 19–40. Cambridge: The MIT Press.

Zeira Yotam, Barbara Parker
      1995 International Joint Ventures in the United States: An Examination of Factors Related to Their Effectiveness. The International Executive 37(4):373–394.

Zhao, Huanxin
      1999 Stance on WTO entry unchanged. China Daily, July 2: 1.

Zheng, Caixiong
      1997 Importance of foreign specialists highlighted. Electronic document,
http://www.chinadaily.net/cndy/history/d2-297.k26.html, accessed, November 26.

Zhang, Yan
      1999 Strategic partnership hailed: Conference stresses importance of joint ventures. China Daily, June 22: 5.

      1999 Companies should improve strategies. China Daily, July 1: 5.